A Hunger for GOD

A Hunger for GOD

What the Bible Really Says About Holiness

EVERETT LEADINGHAM, EDITOR

Though this book is designed for group study, it is also intended
for personal enjoyment and spiritual growth. A leader's guide
is available from your local bookstore or your publisher.

Beacon Hill Press of Kansas City
Kansas City, Missouri

Copyright 2002
by Beacon Hill Press of Kansas City

ISBN: 083-411-9773

Printed in the
United States of America

Editor: Everett Leadingham
Associate Editor: Charlie L. Yourdon
Executive Editor: Larry R. Morris
Writers: Gene Van Note and Stephen M. Miller

Cover design: Ted Ferguson
Cover Photo/Art: PhotoDisc

10   9   8   7   6   5   4   3

Contents

Coming up . . . Living a holy life is the answer to a deep hunger for God. Such a longing can only be satisfied when God's Spirit moves in our lives, making it possible for us to live as His holy people. However, that does not mean we sit passively by—contemplating our navels, if you will—while God does all the work. No, we have a responsibility to seek God as we are driven by our desire to know Him.

How to live a holy life in response to a hunger for God is our theme for the 13 chapters we have before us. We will consider biblical principles that will provide practical guidance on how to live a clean life in a dirty world.

To suggest biblical reasons for holy living implies that there are unscriptural reasons given for living an unholy life. It also raises the question, "Why do people sin?" This foundational chapter comes to grips with that basic question. It will point to the reason sin first entered the moral bloodstream of the human race and why it causes so much trouble to us long after that original sin.

Genesis 3:1-13, 16-19

3 ¹Now the serpent was more crafty than any of the wild animals the LORD God had made. He said to the woman, "Did God really say, 'You must not eat from any tree in the garden'?"

²The woman said to the serpent, "We may eat fruit from the trees in the garden,

³but God did say, 'You must not eat fruit from the tree that is in the middle of the garden, and you must not touch it, or you will die.'"

⁴"You will not surely die," the serpent said to the woman.

⁵"For God knows that when you eat of it your eyes will be opened, and you will be like God, knowing good and evil."

⁶When the woman saw that the fruit of the tree was good for food and pleasing to the eye, and also desirable for gaining wisdom, she took some and ate it. She also gave some to her husband, who was with her, and he ate it.

⁷Then the eyes of both of them were opened, and they realized they were naked; so they sewed fig leaves together and made coverings for themselves.

⁸Then the man and his wife heard the sound of the LORD God as he was walking in the garden in the cool of the day, and they hid from the LORD God among the trees of the garden.

⁹But the LORD God called to the man, "Where are you?"

¹⁰He answered, "I heard you in the garden, and I was afraid because I was naked; so I hid."

¹¹And he said, "Who told you that you were naked? Have you eaten from the tree that I commanded you not to eat from?"

¹²The man said, "The woman you put here with me—she gave me some fruit from the tree, and I ate it."

¹³Then the LORD God said to the woman, "What is this you have done?" The woman said, "The serpent deceived me, and I ate." . . . ¹⁶To the woman he said, "I will greatly increase your pains in childbearing; with pain you will give birth to children. Your desire will be for your husband, and he will rule over you."

¹⁷To Adam he said, "Because you listened to your wife and ate from the tree about which I commanded you, 'You must not eat of it,' Cursed is the ground because of you; through painful toil you will eat of it all the days of your life.

[18]It will produce thorns and thistles for you, and you will eat the plants of the field.

[19]By the sweat of your brow you will eat your food until you return to the ground, since from it you were taken; for dust you are and to dust you will return."

Romans 8:7-8

[7]The sinful mind is hostile to God. It does not submit to God's law, nor can it do so. [8]Those controlled by the sinful nature cannot please God.

1

There's Nothing Original About Sin— but Once There Was!

D O YOU KNOW why people use drugs?" my son asked. "No," I replied.

"Because it's fun," he said.

Eventually drug abuse destroys all that is beautiful and good. However, if drugs were not fun at the beginning, we wouldn't be involved in the worldwide crisis we now experience.

Later, in a quiet place, the conversation with my son sent my mind down a new trail.

Why do people sin?

Because it's fun.

It's been that way since the beginning. That, and what happened when the first couple sinned, is the main concern of this chapter.

Once Sin Was Original
(Genesis 3:1-6)

Is this story in Genesis 3:1-6 a myth, or did it actually happen?

Not much is gained by debating the nationality of the snake, the kind of fruit produced by the tree, or the geographical location of the Garden of Eden. The New Testament treats it as an actual event. A vital Christian doctrine is based on it as fact. That's good enough for us.

Make no mistake, however, it is a powerful story with a devastating conclusion. Yet, since most of us are not able to read Genesis in the original Hebrew language, there are subtleties we can easily overlook. A little time spent in word study will pay rich dividends in understanding this important passage.

"The LORD God made the earth and the heavens" (Genesis 2:4, emphasis added). This Hebrew couplet, "LORD God," is found 20 times in Genesis, especially in chapters 2 and 3. Modern translations, such as the NIV and the RSV place "LORD" in small capital letters to identify the significance of the word and show the difference between "LORD" and "God." It will help us to try and understand the difference between the Hebrew words translated "LORD" and "God."[1]

In English, LORD is used when the Hebrew uses the personal name for God—Yahweh (YAH-way). Yahweh is the One who revealed himself to Abram when He established the covenant (Genesis 15:7). Yahweh is the one who met Moses at the burning bush to reaffirm the covenant and send him back to Egypt (Exodus 3:1 and following). Yahweh is the covenant-partner, the personal God of salvation-history. Yahweh is the only God, not the chief of gods.

God, as used here in Genesis 2, is the Hebrew word Elohim (el-oh-HEEM), referring to the God of power who created all things. Elohim is often used of heathen gods as well as the one true God who demanded the exclusive allegiance of the Hebrews. When the sacred writer wrote this couplet, "the LORD God," he was saying something the Hebrews would have quickly understood and we so easily miss. The personal God of salvation-history is the God who created humans to walk in fellowship with Him.

Are you still with me? I hope so, because the implications of this word study are vital to understanding the original sin.

"[The serpent] said to the woman, 'Did God really say . . . ?' The woman said to the serpent, 'We may eat fruit from the trees in the garden, but *God* did say . . .'" (3:1-3, emphasis added).

Notice the subtle but significant change. In Genesis 2, it was the LORD God who made all things, including man and woman. Yet when the serpent talked to the woman and she answered, neither used the name of the personal God of salvation-history but the name of God in general. Eve has taken the serpent's bait and swallowed it hook, line, and sinker! The personal God of intimate fellowship was reduced to the remote God of power. We know from personal experience how much easier it is to reject persons when we can put some distance between us and them.

"When the woman saw that the fruit of the tree was good for food and pleasing to the eye, . . . she took some and ate it. She also gave some to her husband . . . and he ate it" (3:6). Trouble followed. It was more serious than indigestion from eating green apples. That original sin was caused by removing God from the throne of the human heart. Both Adam and Eve had succumbed to the temptation to become gods themselves.

"Eve listened to a creature instead of the Creator, followed her impressions against her instructions, and made self-fulfillment her goal. . . . But [humanity's] lifeline is spiritual, namely God's Word and the response of faith; to break it is death."[2]

Once, sin was original, and humanity was never again the same afterward.

A Pattern Revealed
(Genesis 3:7-13, 16-19)

"Did God really say, 'You must not eat from any tree in the garden'?" the crafty serpent asked (3:1). It was a clever question, worthy of his reputation.

"Did God really say?" Can you hear the sound of the serpent's voice? A sense of unbelief carries the question along. Almost as if he said, "I just can't believe God really meant for you not to have the pleasure of all the good trees He placed in the garden. Do you really think that's what God meant?"

For the first time, Eve learned it was possible to doubt God. Not deny Him. Just question or second-guess Him.

She supported the Creator's instructions, but it was a halfhearted defense. "The woman said to the serpent, 'We may eat fruit from the trees in the garden, *but God did say . . .*'" (3:2-3, emphasis added).

Eve not only doubted but also added a restriction that does not appear earlier in the text: "But God did say . . . 'you must not touch it, or you will die'" (3:3). She had been drawn into the discussion of the possibility of sin on the tempter's terms. Eve's attention had turned from the LORD God to the tree, and whether or not God is fair.

The serpent's initial thrust had been successful.

"'You will not surely die,' the serpent said to the woman. 'For God knows that when you eat of it . . . you will be like God'" (3:4-5). Now, it's the serpent's word against God. "To be as God, and achieve it by outwitting Him is intoxicating."[3]

Sin gains momentum as the "LORD God" becomes "God," and then merely "god." Humans desire to be elevated to godlike status because of the attractiveness of sin. "When the woman saw that the fruit of the tree was good for food and pleasing to the eye, and also desirable for gaining wisdom, she took some and ate it. She also gave some to her husband, who was with her, and he ate it" (3:6).

From that moment on, God and humanity found themselves on opposite sides of a wide gulf. Surely Eve didn't think it was all that significant. "She took some and ate it." However, "so simple the act, so hard its undoing. God will taste poverty and death before 'take and eat' become verbs of salvation."[4]

Once, sin was original. Eve, and then Adam, did something they had never done before. The creatures had rejected the Creator. The sovereign God had been dethroned.

Yet, thrones don't stay vacant. Someone sits there. God was replaced by a human. Adam and Eve not only rejected the Creator, they took possession of the throne. By responding favorably to the enticing words of the serpent, they placed themselves "under the lordship of self. . . . The exaltation of self to the control tower of life . . . perverts man's relation to everything—himself, others, and God."[5]

Sin Is No Longer Original
(Romans 8:7-8)

There is a distressing monotony to sin. Read the pages of the newspaper, and you'll be subjected to a daily barrage of rapes and murders, theft and violence, burglary and embezzlement. Go to work, and you'll be pressured to compromise your ethical standards for the "good of the company." Even at church we've not always successfully combated the temptations of gossip, character assassination, and competition for power. Across the generations, men and women have created new toys and new technology. These have changed the face but not the character of sin.

Romans 8:7-8 tells us why. Here the RSV gives us a most helpful translation: "For the mind that is set on the flesh is hostile to God; it does not submit to God's law, indeed it cannot; and those who are in the flesh cannot please God." Theologians call this mind-set and hostility "original sin." John Wesley explained it this way,

> Man was created looking directly to God . . . but, falling into sin, he . . . turned into himself. Now, this infers a total apostasy and universal corruption in man; for where the last end is changed there can be no real goodness. And this is the case of all men in their natural state. They seek not God, but themselves.[6]

The repetition of the word "cannot" in Romans 8:7-8 should do more than capture our attention. It should frighten us. Surely, as clever as we are, there is something we can do to please God. But the apostle Paul says no. In our sinful condition, apart from the cleansing power of the Holy Spirit, we can neither please God nor submit to His law. That is because sin is dual in nature. We sin because we commit acts of sin and are sinners from birth because of the original sin in the garden that changed forever both humanity's relation to God and our inner nature.

Why should this be? One theologian answers it like this:

> To live at the level of animal appetites and merely human desires . . . is to live where the law is impotent precisely because the mind-set is away from God; it is to live where sin is able to bind closely to death because the one power (of God) which can defeat sin's power has been thrown off.[7]

Paul contrasts the seriousness of sin and the possibility of salvation for us in another great passage in Romans. "Therefore, just as sin entered the world through one man, and death through sin . . . so also through the obedience of the one man the many will be made righteous" (5:12, 19). The sacrificial death of Christ on the Cross provides for both the forgiveness of the sins we commit and the cleansing of our sinful nature that prompts the moral misdeeds.

Personal awareness of the tragedy of our sinful state is, surprisingly, the door to a holy life. We can begin nowhere else.

Notes:

1. This discussion leans heavily on C. F. Keil and F. Delitzsch, *Commentary on the Old Testament*, vol. 1 (Grand Rapids: William B. Eerdmans Publishing Company, 1978), 72-76, and Gordon J. Wenham, *Genesis 1—15*, vol. 1 of *Word Biblical Commentary* (Waco, Tex.: Word Books, 1987), 88-89.

2. Derek Kidner, *Genesis*, vol. 1 of *Tyndale Old Testament Commentaries* (London: Tyndale Press, 1967), 68.

3. Kidner, 68.

4. Kidner, 68.

5. H. Ray Dunning, *Grace, Faith, and Holiness* (Kansas City: Beacon Hill Press of Kansas City, 1988), 293-94.

6. William M. Greathouse and H. Ray Dunning, *An Introduction to Wesleyan Theology* (Kansas City: Beacon Hill Press of Kansas City, 1989), 55.

7. James D. G. Dunn, *Romans 1—8*, vol. 38A of *Word Biblical Commentary* (Dallas: Word Books, 1988), 443.

Word to Remember: *The sinful mind is hostile to God. It does not submit to God's law, nor can it do so* (Romans 8:7).

Coming Up . . . In the previous chapter, we took a close look at the event in the Garden of Eden that changed forever humanity's relation to a holy God. That original sin was more than a one-time happening, however. Adam and Eve were evicted from the garden and kept out by a flaming sword. Deprived of the presence of God, they became depraved. Not only were they sinners by their actions, they became sinners by nature. Without hope, they needed a savior. The promise came quickly. "The LORD God said to the serpent . . . I will put enmity between you and the woman, and between your offspring and hers; he will crush your head, and you will strike his heel" (Genesis 3:14-15).

This early promise of redemption was fulfilled in Christ, as we will see in this chapter. And as we will see later on in the book, Christ came not only to set right the wrong done in the garden, but to restore completely the relationship humanity had with God. By living Christlike lives —that is, lives of holiness—we share once again in the beautiful plan for fellowship God designed for us.

Hebrews 10:1-18

10 ¹The law is only a shadow of the good things that are coming—not the realities themselves. For this reason it can never, by the same sacrifices repeated endlessly year after year, make perfect those who draw near to worship. ²If it could, would they not have stopped being offered? For the worshipers would have been cleansed once for all, and would no longer have felt guilty for their sins. ³But those sacrifices are an annual reminder of sins, ⁴because it is impossible for the blood of bulls and goats to take away sins.

⁵Therefore, when Christ came into the world, he said: "Sacrifice and offering you did not desire, but a body you prepared for me; ⁶with burnt offerings and sin offerings you were not pleased. ⁷Then I said, 'Here I am—it is written about me in the scroll—I have come to do your will, O God.'" ⁸First he said, "Sacrifices and offerings, burnt offerings and sin offerings you did not desire, nor were you pleased with them" (although the law required them to be made). ⁹Then he said, "Here I am, I have come to do your will." He sets aside the first to establish the second. ¹⁰And by that will, we have been made holy through the sacrifice of the body of Jesus Christ once for all.

¹¹Day after day every priest stands and performs his religious duties; again and again he offers the same sacrifices, which can never take away sins. ¹²But when this priest had offered for all time one sacrifice for sins, he sat down at the right hand of God. ¹³Since that time he waits for his enemies to be made his footstool, ¹⁴because by one sacrifice he has made perfect forever those who are being made holy.

¹⁵The Holy Spirit also testifies to us about this. First he says: ¹⁶"This is the covenant I will make with them after that time, says the Lord. I will put my laws in their hearts, and I will write them on their minds." ¹⁷Then he adds: "Their sins and lawless acts I will remember no more." ¹⁸And where these have been forgiven, there is no longer any sacrifice for sin.

2

Practice Doesn't Always Make Perfect

"**P**RACTICE makes perfect." These were the words my mother used to get me to practice my piano lessons. Those three words were also hurled at me in a variety of other activities that adults wanted me to practice—football, writing, even washing the family car.

However, I have come to doubt the truth of that famous adage. I practiced the piano scales, but I never really learned to play. I played lots of football, but I didn't get any better. Left to my own devices, I simply practiced the same mistakes over and over. If I had not looked elsewhere for examples of good writing, I would have kept on until I was a proficient *bad* writer. And we don't even need to talk about the tons of dirt I left on the family car!

If, in fact, practice makes perfect, then the ancient Hebrews should have arrived, for they practiced their religion with great diligence. However, they learned that it takes more than continued repetition to bring happiness and release from guilt. That's why this chapter is so important. We, too, know what it means to practice our religion vigorously and still be empty.

Bulls and Goats—Impossible
(Hebrews 10:1-4)

Hebrews 10:1-4 is a tough passage for most of us. We have no quarrel with the words, "It is impossible for the blood of bulls and goats to take away sins" (v. 4). We never thought it did.

Nevertheless, the ancient disciples of Moses did seek forgiveness by making animal sacrifices in the Temple. Not only because that is what they had been taught to believe, but also it was written in the holy book. "The LORD said to Moses, . . . 'For the life of a creature is in the blood, and I have given it to you to make atonement for yourselves on the altar; it is the blood that makes atonement for one's life'" (Leviticus 17:1, 11).

The Hebrews writer gave three reasons why "the same sacrifices repeated endlessly year after year [can never] make perfect those who draw near to worship" (10:1). Let's look at his reasoning.

"If it could, would they not have stopped being offered?" (10:2).

The Hebrew performing the rituals spelled out in the Mosaic Law was not like the coach who says to his players, "We're going to keep doing this until we get it right." Nor was he like the coaches at halftime who say to each other, "Our pregame plans didn't work, what can we do now?"

Certainly there was some satisfaction and release in the daily sacrifices and the great rituals on the Day of Atonement. But no permanent joy. No freedom from sin and sinning.

"If it could . . . the worshipers would have been cleansed once for all, and would no longer have felt guilty for their sins" (10:2).

We've been exposed to enough psychology to know that sometimes people feel guilty when they haven't done anything wrong. It's called "false guilt." Yet, we've also lived long enough to know what real guilt is, and how good it feels to be free from it. The Law never provided that freedom. In spite of the magnificent ceremony and the costly sacrifices, the guilt was not erased.

"Those sacrifices are an annual reminder of sins" (10:3).

A terrible sadness is wrapped up in these words. The God-given rituals designed to provide atonement served also as a reminder that the ceremonies were inadequate. The endless repetition haunted those who would be righteous in the sight of God. Consider how empty a devout high priest must have felt when he sprinkled blood on the mercy seat in the holy of holies. If he looked closely through the smoke of the incense, he could see the fresh blood falling on the stains of last year's sacrifice.

Is it any wonder the writer of Hebrews wrote, "It is impossible for the blood of bulls and goats to take away sins" (10:4)?

Therefore ... Christ Came
(Hebrews 10:5-10)

Did you ever do just exactly what you were told to do and then find out it wasn't good enough? I suspect most of us have been in that position at one time or another. That was the plight of those who tried to follow the Mosaic Law to salvation.

Here, again, the words from Hebrews are more difficult for us to understand than they would have been for the first readers. So, let's take it a step at a time.

Step 1: "When Christ came into the world, he said: 'Sacrifice and offering you did not desire'" (10:5). These words are only part of the story, but they are a vital part.

When Jesus said that the Father was not happy with the sacrifices and offerings of the covenant people, He was repeating a theme that winds like a dark thread through the Old Testament. Often the prophets said the same thing.

Samuel said, "Does the LORD delight in burnt offerings and sacrifices as much as in obeying the voice of the LORD?" (1 Samuel 15:22). David cried out in penitence, "The sacrifices of God are a broken spirit; a broken and contrite heart, O God, you will not despise" (Psalm 51:17). Hosea proclaimed the words of the Lord, "For I desire mercy, not sacrifice, and acknowledgment of God rather than burnt offerings" (Hosea 6:6).

Among the covenant people, the most devout struggled to find a way to please God. For the majority, ritual had become meaningless formality.

Step 2: "I have come to do your will, O God'" (Hebrews 10:7). This statement is more easily understood in relation to the life of Christ than to the ancient system of seeking salvation through animal sacrifice. We have read how our Lord submitted to the will of the Father in that dramatic scene in the Garden of Gethsemane (Matthew 26:39).

However, the writer to the Hebrews has clearly placed our Lord against the backdrop of the past. Are we to understand these words to say that, prior to Christ, no one was ready and able to do God's will? A yes answer to this question would be unfair to hosts of devout people who lived before Jesus was born in Bethlehem's cattle stall. Ready, but not able, would be more accurate. Only Jesus was fully able to meet the demands of God's love, justice, and holiness in relation to humanity's sin. A new step had been taken in human redemption that only Christ could take. The Hebrews writer gave us a hint how that took place.

Step 3: "By [God's] will, we have been made holy through the sacrifice of the body of Jesus Christ once for all" (10:10). This picks up a theme expressed earlier in verse 5, "Sacrifice and offering you did not desire, but a body you prepared for me." These words properly focus our attention on the centrality of the Cross in our redemption.

Herein lies, also, the foundational truth on which these chapters on living a holy life are based. Any moral cleanness we may experience is based entirely on the sacred truth that the Son of God became one of us. Our holiness is completely dependent on the obedience of Jesus Christ, the God-Man. As the NASB puts Hebrews 10:10, "We have been sanctified through the offering of the body of Jesus Christ once for all."

"Of course," writes one scholar, "what the writer [of Hebrews] is saying is not that believers have no further need of obedience because Christ has accomplished it, but that God received us on the basis of Christ's perfect fulfillment of His will"*

By One Sacrifice
(Hebrews 10:11-18)

The verses in Hebrews 10:11-18 are closely connected to the preceding verses. They are not the beginning of a new idea but a continuation of all we have considered so far in this chapter.

"Every priest stands" (10:11). "[Christ] sat down" (10:12). What a dramatic contrast! Priests, with tired feet, endlessly repeating ineffective sacrifices "which can never take away sins" (10:11). Jesus Christ at rest, His mission completed.

Wrapped up in the formal language of Hebrews is the transforming truth of Christianity—Jesus' grave was not the end. Christ is alive! However, His return from the shrouds of death was not like Lazarus, who was reunited with his sisters only to face death once again at some unknown date. "When this priest [Jesus Christ] had offered for all time one sacrifice for sins, he sat down at the right hand of God" (10:12).

"By one sacrifice he has made perfect forever those who are being made holy" (10:14). Or, as it is translated in the NASB, "For by one offering He has perfected for all time those who are sanctified." Since the word in the original Greek is in the present tense, some translations have "being sanctified" to pick up the continuous nature of our sanctification, that is, the process of continuing to live a holy life.

Perfection, and how to obtain it, is a central theme in the Book of Hebrews. In this climactic moment in Hebrews, the writer makes it clear that any perfection we can ever know results from the "once for all" sacrifice of Jesus. We need to hear this truth as much as the first-century Hebrew Christians. In fact, it may be easier and more tempting for us to believe we can save ourselves. If not through politics, at least through education and science. The writer to the Hebrews would have none of that. We are sanctified only through the grace of God.

What does the phrase "being sanctified" mean? As we will see when we study 1 Thessalonians in chapter 4, it does not dispute the crisis moment known as entire sanctification. The question raised by Bible scholars is this: Does "being sanctified" refer to the continuous action of God's grace in each individual Christian? Or does it identify the long succession of Christians through the ages who have been sanctified?

As we proceed through this book, we will note on many occasions that our sanctification involves both cleansing and maturing. So, in that sense, sanctification is both complete and incomplete at the same time—depending on what aspect we are emphasizing.

Gratefully, we can also affirm that God's grace that makes "perfect forever those who are being made holy" cannot be depleted. We can pump oil wells dry, but we can never exhaust the sanctifying grace of God.

Before we are finished, we need to ask one more question: Why did the writer keep repeating the idea that Christ's sacrifice was the only way to salvation?

Here we are forced to speculate a bit, and our answer takes us beyond these scripture passages. Most likely, the writer to the Hebrews knew that some of his readers were being tempted to believe there was some possibility of salvation in the old ways. They were tempted to return to the pageantry of the Temple, to the traditions of their fathers.

Animal sacrifices don't attract us, but sometimes the old ways of this world do. The Bible here shouts one answer to that temptation—Christ alone provides the means for attaining holiness of heart and life. We need to pay attention to that message as much as any generation in history.

Notes:

*Donald Guthrie, *Hebrews,* vol. 15 of *Tyndale New Testament Commentaries* (Grand Rapids: William B. Eerdmans Publishing Company, 1983), 206.

Word to Remember: *Because by one sacrifice he has made perfect forever those who are being made holy* (Hebrews 10:14).

Coming up . . . Quite candidly, the first promise of salvation is a bit hard for us to grasp: "The LORD God said to the serpent . . . I will put enmity between you and the woman, and between your offspring and hers; he will crush your head, and you will strike his heel" (Genesis 3:14-15). As sacred history unfolds in the pages of the Bible, the message of salvation becomes easier to understand. It is never predictable, however. The people who lived when Jesus lived heard Him talk, watched Him heal, and kept getting off track. You'd think that after nearly 2,000 years we would do better. Still, we keep getting sidetracked at many of the same places they did. Often the problem is not an inability to hear but an unwillingness to accept Jesus at face value. That's our challenge in this chapter, as we lay another block in the foundation on which we will try to build a holy life.

Luke 14:25-35

14 [25]Large crowds were traveling with Jesus, and turning to them he said: [26]"If anyone comes to me and does not hate his father and mother, his wife and children, his brothers and sisters— yes, even his own life—he cannot be my disciple. [27]And anyone who does not carry his cross and follow me cannot be my disciple.

[28]"Suppose one of you wants to build a tower. Will he not first sit down and estimate the cost to see if he has enough money to complete it? [29]For if he lays the foundation and is not able to finish it, everyone who sees it will ridicule him, [30]saying, 'This fellow began to build and was not able to finish.'

[31]"Or suppose a king is about to go to war against another king. Will he not first sit down and consider whether he is able with ten thousand men to oppose the one coming against him with twenty thousand? [32]If he is not able, he will send a delegation while the other is still a long way off and will ask for terms of peace. [33]In the same way, any of you who does not give up everything he has cannot be my disciple.

[34]"Salt is good, but if it loses its saltiness, how can it be made salty again? [35]It is fit neither for the soil nor for the manure pile; it is thrown out.

"He who has ears to hear, let him hear."

3

Count the Cost/
Discount the Cost

IN A FEW WEEKS Jesus would be dead.

Yet, there was no smell of death in the air on the Sabbath Jesus was invited to a prominent Pharisee's home for dinner (Luke 14:1). Jesus was on His way to Jerusalem. No fanfare. No marching bands. No press agents. No advance party to whip up enthusiasm. None of that because none was needed. A friend told a friend who told two others, and soon thousands scrambled to see the miracle-working Galilean (see Luke 12:1).

Patiently or impatiently, we don't know, the crowd waited outside the Pharisee's home until the meal was over. Then they rejoined Christ on His journey to the Holy City.

It is not hard to conclude what the crowd had on its mind. That is, if Christ's closest friends give us any clue at all. Not much later, Jesus heard them arguing about who was to have first place in His kingdom—His earthly kingdom, of course (22:24).

Perhaps it's also possible to figure out what Jesus was thinking. Could it be that He said to himself, "They suppose I'm going to Jerusalem to launch a revolution, but they're wrong. A cross, not a crown, is at the end of this road"? And so our Lord spoke to the crowd to help them grasp His mission. There is no reason to believe they understood what they heard because it was a hard saying. Not one they wanted to hear.

We are no different. Yet, if we are to be followers of the Lord Jesus Christ, we must not only hear these words but heed them. That will not be easy for they are some of the most challenging, most difficult words He ever spoke.

A Disciple Must Choose to Hate
(Luke 14:25-27)

Rarely do we have a greater desire to "explain" Jesus than in Luke 14:25-27. Surely He could not have meant what He said. Of course, we believe the Bible, but does Jesus really want us to hate people? We want to find ways to dodge these verses because, if we can't, then following Jesus means something different from what we want it to mean. If these words must be taken at face value, then we will likely respond as the disciples did in another place, "Who then can be saved?" (Matthew 19:25).

Hate who? Just who is it we are called on to hate? Those who are closest and dearest to us:

- father and mother
- wife and children
- brothers and sisters
- ourselves.

Jesus said that if anyone comes to Him and will not hate all these people, he or she "cannot be my disciple" (14:26).

Perhaps we can use a method some preachers employ when the English translation is tough to understand or difficult to accept. Let's ask the question, "What does the original Greek word mean?" You shouldn't have asked. The word in the original is "an old and very strong verb [which means] to hate or detest."[1]

How can a God of love command us to hate? This is the same Jesus who said, "Honor your father and mother, and love your neighbor as yourself" (Matthew 19:19). And, "Love your enemies, do good to those who hate you" (Luke 6:27).

Looks like we have an impossible situation: love our enemies but hate our families if we want to be His disciples.

What, then, does "hate" mean in these verses?

We got off the track too soon in our word study. The verb that originally meant "to detest" is used sometimes in the New Testament to mean "to regard with less affection, love less, esteem less. Matthew 6:24 and Luke 14:26 are two examples of the word used this way."[2]

Though true, this is a dangerous definition. It's like the tax laws. There are too many loopholes. We find so many reasons to explain away our partial commitment to the cause of Christ and our small involvement in the ministry of the Body of Christ.

"Hating" our loved ones for the privilege of being called Christians is far more than singing some catchy little ditty like, "I'm going to love Him better every day." Jesus said it was taking up our cross and following Him (14:27). That doesn't mean much to us. Our crosses are gold-plated, handsome trinkets on a chain. People treat them like an amulet to ward off evil spirits.

Christ's hearers knew what it meant to carry a cross, however. They had seen people, perhaps their family or friends, carrying the heavy timber that would become the instrument of their execution. It wasn't pretty. It wasn't easy. It didn't make friends with people in prominent places. It was definitely hazardous to one's health! Those early Christians who scratched the sign of a cross on the walls of the catacombs alongside a crudely drawn fish knew about the Cross. And they knew something about the scandal of the Cross, from which we shrink. Yet Jesus said, "Anyone who does not carry his cross and follow me cannot be my disciple."

Gradually it comes into focus. The command to hate is not an excuse to be a nasty person. Nor is dedication to Christ like those who cry, "Kill the infidel!" It is a call to love God supremely, and then, strengthened by that, love the world compassionately and without discrimination.

A missionary, his wife, and two children arrived back in the United States on furlough only a few days before his home church had their annual missionary convention. They had spent four years in a country torn by civil war. Though they lived in a "safe" part of the capital city, they never left their home after dark because it was too dangerous. When the ushers distributed the pledge cards, the missionary wrote in the space that called for the amount to be given: "Four more years."

Four more years away from aging parents. Four more years of daily exposure to the terrorism that invaded even their quiet residential neighborhood. Four more years of humble service for Christ in a bleeding, war-ravaged country.

This is the way a disciple must choose to hate. It is a hard word, but it is the Lord's word.

A Disciple Must Have the Courage to Count
(Luke 14:28-33)

A young couple sat on the porch of a mountain resort, watching the evening sun set over a peaceful lake. He took her in his arms and began to speak quietly to her. Just around the corner, an elderly couple sat, more interested in the scene on the porch than the reflected glory of the sun on the water.

"Joe," the wife whispered," he's going to propose to her. Whistle to warn."

"Nobody warned me not to propose," the old codger replied.

Life's like that. Think of the number of times you've said, "This isn't what I counted on." Or, "If I'd known it was going to turn out like this, I never would have done it." Most of us make most of our decisions rather impulsively. No doubt that's why Jesus took the time to illustrate His hard saying.

A tower and a war. Two timeless little stories that teach us as effectively as they did when Christ first told them. We don't see many half-finished buildings. Yet, we all know someone who tried to start a small business and didn't anticipate all the hidden costs. And we have heard about the costly consequences of battles left unfinished.

These two little stories remind us that Christ is not happy with "jaunty discipleship and impulsive loyalty."[3] He asks those who would be His followers to count the cost. We have already noted in this study part of the cost of being a disciple of Christ. To love Christ so much all other loves seem like hatred is an all-encompassing love. Jesus put it another way: "Any of you who does not give up everything he has cannot be my disciple" (14:33). People react differently to this kind of sweeping request. Some, like the rich young man, listen respectfully then leave quietly. "He went away sad, because he had great wealth" (Mark 10:22).

John wrote about a time when the crowd became disenchanted with Jesus. "From this time many of his disciples turned back and no longer followed him" (6:66). Then the Lord turned to His closest followers and asked, "You do not want to leave too, do you?" (v. 67).

"Simon Peter answered him, 'Lord, to whom shall we go? You have the words of eternal life'" (v. 68). Yet, with all these brave words, the night came when he gave voice to almost forgotten fisherman's oaths in the courtyard of the high priest.

Jesus said, "Count the cost!"

Two stories with one meaning—almost. The tower and the war story seem to be saying the same thing: count the cost. Yet, there is a subtle difference pointed out in these words:

> The builder of the tower is free to build or not as he chooses, but the king is being invaded. He must do something. In the first parable, Jesus says, "Sit down and reckon whether you can afford to follow me." In the second, He says, "Sit down and reckon whether you can afford to refuse my demands."[4]

It doesn't get any easier does it? Jesus said that only when a disciple has chosen to hate and counted the cost can he or she be judged worthy.

A Disciple Changes the World
(Luke 14:34-35)

Salt. It's everywhere. It sharpens the taste of our food, freezes ice cream faster, preserves meat, makes icy roads less hazardous and heart doctors nervous. Gargle with it if you have a sore throat; mix it with soda and brush your teeth. Sodium chloride (chemical formula: NaCl) is everywhere.

Salt has been used across the centuries to confirm covenants. It has been a part of religious ceremonies, and an expression of friendship. The modern English word "salary" is derived from the Latin, salarium, which originally referred to the direct payment of salt as wages to soldiers.

Salt, in ancient times, was not pure. Sodium chloride is always sodium chloride, but the salt reclaimed from the Dead Sea had other chemicals mixed with it, primarily gypsum. This impure salt could lose its salty taste if water leached the sodium chloride away.

On the negative side, Jesus taught that halfhearted disciples were like salt with the sodium chloride gone. This product didn't have limited value. It had no value!

On the positive side, a disciple has as much influence on the world as salt. Good salt. Pure sodium chloride. Salt does its work quietly. Not like the roar of a fire, the thunder of a waterfall, or the smashing impact of lightning. Unseen, salt works to change its world.

Christians are like that. True disciples of Jesus change their world by the subtle influence of their good lives and sweet spirit. Those who stood by the open grave of a Christian teenager said, "It was easier to be good when she was around." The world should be able to say that about everyone who claims to follow Jesus.

Notes:

1. Archibald T. Robertson, *Word Pictures in the New Testament* (Nashville: Broadman Press, 1930), 200.

2. *The Analytical Greek Lexicon* (New York: Harper, n.d.).

3. *Luke, John*, vol. 8 of *The Interpreter's Bible* (Nashville: Abingdon Press, 1952), 261.

4. Leon Morris, *Luke*, vol. 3 of *Tyndale New Testament Commentaries* (Grand Rapids: William B. Eerdmans Publishing Company, 1984), 236.

Word to Remember: In the same way, any of you who does not give up everything he has cannot be my disciple (Luke 14:33).

Coming up . . . Our challenge in this series of Bible studies is to explore what it means to live the holy life. We began with the self-evident observation that you don't need to clean something unless it is dirty. Humans are morally dirty. Adam and Eve's original sin forever changed everyone's relation to a holy God. We are sinners both by who we are and what we have done—we sin because we are sinful by nature. However, God moved to restore this broken relationship, making full redemption possible through the sacrifice of Jesus on the Cross. Release from sin and sinning is not automatic, however. We must respond by making a full commitment to follow Him. In the last chapter, we looked at Christ's command that we count the cost before making our decision. In this chapter, we will see that the salvation He provided on the Cross offers forgiveness from sins committed and makes possible cleansing from our sinful nature.

I Thessalonians 1:3-10

1 [3]We continually remember before our God and Father your work produced by faith, your labor prompted by love, and your endurance inspired by hope in our Lord Jesus Christ.

[4]For we know, brothers loved by God, that he has chosen you, [5]because our gospel came to you not simply with words, but also with power, with the Holy Spirit and with deep conviction. You know how we lived among you for your sake. [6]You became imitators of us and of the Lord; in spite of severe suffering, you welcomed the message with the joy given by the Holy Spirit. [7]And so you became a model to all the believers in Macedonia and Achaia. [8]The Lord's message rang out from you not only in Macedonia and Achaia—your faith in God has become known everywhere. Therefore we do not need to say anything about it, [9]for they themselves report what kind of reception you gave us. They tell how you turned to God from idols to serve the living and true God, [10]and to wait for his Son from heaven, whom he raised from the dead—Jesus, who rescues us from the coming wrath.

I Thessalonians 4:1-12

4 [1]Finally, brothers, we instructed you how to live in order to please God, as in fact you are living. Now we ask you and urge you in the Lord Jesus to do this more and more. [2]For you know what instructions we gave you by the authority of the Lord Jesus.

[3]It is God's will that you should be sanctified: that you should avoid sexual immorality; [4]that each of you should learn to control his own body in a way that is holy and honorable, [5]not in passionate lust like the heathen, who do not know God; [6]and that in this matter no one should wrong his brother or take advantage of him. The Lord will punish men for all such sins, as we have already told you and warned you. [7]For God did not call us to be impure, but to live a holy life. [8]Therefore, he who rejects this instruction does not reject man but God, who gives you his Holy Spirit.

[9]Now about brotherly love we do not need to write to you, for you yourselves have been taught by God to love each other. [10]And in fact, you do love all the brothers throughout Macedonia. Yet we urge you, brothers, to do so more and more.

[11]Make it your ambition to lead a quiet life, to mind your own business and to work with your hands, just as we told you,

[12]so that your daily life may win the respect of outsiders and so that you will not be dependent on anybody.

I Thessalonians 5:23-24

5 [23]May God himself, the God of peace, sanctify you through and through. May your whole spirit, soul and body be kept blameless at the coming of our Lord Jesus Christ. [24]The one who calls you is faithful and he will do it.

4

The Thessalonian Model for Holy Living

THE CITY OF Thessalonica, Salonika as it is now known, was located in northern Greece. Salonika has a current population approaching a half-million people and is the best seaport in southeast Europe.

Thessalonica was founded in 315 B.C. by the Macedonian general Cassander, who named the city after his wife. She was the daughter of Philip and stepsister of Alexander the Great. Refugees from many surrounding towns and cities that had been destroyed in war settled the city.

The apostle Paul on his second missionary journey founded the Christian church in Thessalonica (Acts 17:1-4). Most of what we know about that Early Church comes from the letters Paul wrote, which we know as First and Second Thessalonians. They may be the first letters we have from the pen of Paul, and may be the first part of the New Testament to be written.

About 20 years after Christ's death and resurrection, Paul, Silas, and their young friend Timothy sailed west from Troas on one of the most important trips in history. A few weeks later, after the conversion of a slave girl in Philippi, the city authorities had them "stripped and beaten. After they had been severely flogged, they were thrown into prison" (Acts 16:22-23). After the same magistrates learned that Paul and Silas were Roman citizens, "they were alarmed. They came to appease them and escorted them from the prison" (16:39). Then those officials "politely" asked them to leave town. The pioneer missionaries then traveled a few miles west to the key city of Thessalonica.

Once again, they were successful evangelists. "Many of the Jews believed, as did also a number of prominent Greek women and many Greek men" (17:12). However, they were not treated as "kindly" as they had been in Philippi. Some Jews rented a mob and chased them out of town.

Athens was the next stop for Paul. Later, Silas and Timothy joined him in Corinth. In the meantime, Paul had preached to the philosophers in Athens, and Timothy had gone back to Thessalonica to see how the Christians were doing. Timothy's optimistic report prompted Paul to write a letter. This short, friendly letter gives us another view of what it means to live a holy life.

They Were Believers
(1 Thessalonians 1:3-10)

Sometimes missionaries get discouraged. I know that statement goes contrary to the myths we have about missionaries, that they are super-human and not subject to the same emotions we have. Yet, even missionaries have the blues once in a while. Paul did.

That's one of the reasons he couldn't relax in Athens. The paganism disturbed him. He also wondered if his beachhead in Thessalonica had been washed away by Satan's high tides. That's why Timothy went back. When he rejoined Paul in Corinth, he was bubbling with enthusiasm because of what he had seen and heard.

The Thessalonians who received Paul's letter were Christian believers. Note these excerpts from chapter 1:

- "We continually remember . . . your work produced by faith, your labor prompted by love, and your endurance inspired by hope in our Lord Jesus Christ" (v. 3).
- Paul called them, "brothers" (v. 4).
- "You became imitators of us and of the Lord; in spite of severe suffering, you welcomed the message with the joy given by the Holy Spirit" (v. 6).

- "You became a model to all the believers in Macedonia and Achaia" (v. 7).
- "The Lord's message rang out from you" (v. 8).
- "Your faith in God has become known everywhere. . . . They tell how you turned to God from idols to serve the living and true God, and to wait for his Son from heaven" (vv. 8-10).

Let's explore those phrases and look at them a piece at a time.

- *Faith, love, and hope in our Lord Jesus Christ.* That's high praise from the apostle.
- *Brothers.* This word, in singular or plural form, is used 28 times in Paul's two short letters to the Thessalonians. The once-proud Jewish nationalist had close ties with these Greeks because of their common love of Jesus.
- *Imitators of us and of the Lord.* Indeed, their reputation as models of the Christian faith was so well-known in that part of the world Paul did not have to tell anyone about them.
- *The Lord's message rang out.* A picturesque word that can also be used for the sound of a trumpet or the roll of thunder. The Thessalonians had not hidden their testimony in a closet.
- *Turned from idols to serve the living and true God.* Among first-century Greeks, this was an extremely important piece of evidence that marked a true Christian.
- *Wait for His Son from heaven.* With keen expectation they were looking for Christ's return from glory and in glory.

The conclusion is inescapable: the Thessalonians had come to know Jesus as their personal Savior and continued in that faith.

They Were Called to Holy Living
(I Thessalonians 4:1-12)

It used to be harder for some of us to understand ancient Greece than it is now. Once we were shocked by what the ancients did. Things like hiring a prostitute as a banquet companion and leaving the wife at home. Disregarding marital vows when it was convenient. Divorcing a spouse when marriage became inconvenient. Exposing infant children to die if they were the wrong sex or came at an inopportune time. Spending money for a wide variety of morally degrading forms of entertainment.

Now all we need to do is sit in front of our television sets.

God called the Christians in Thessalonica to live morally clean lives in an incredibly dirty world. "God's plan is to make you holy," J. B. Phillips translates 4:3, "and that entails first of all a clean cut with sexual immorality."

The Thessalonian believers were out of step with their world. That's old news, but unless we keep it up front in our thinking, we cannot understand the radical nature of Paul's commands. Read verses 3-8 aloud and feel the power of the apostle's words. His hearers were to set their priorities by God's standards, not the world's.

The apostle also insisted that holy living was not optional for a Christian. Actually the words in 4:1, "how to live in order to please God," could properly be translated, "how you must live in order to please God."

Holy living involves far more than sexual purity. In first-century Thessalonica, this was the most visible point of tension between Christianity and the local pagan religions. Holy living touches every nook and cranny of our lives. "The calling of God is not to impurity but to the most thorough purity, and anyone who makes light of the matter is not making light of a man's ruling but of God's command. It is not for nothing that the Spirit God gives us is called the Holy Spirit" (4:7-8, PHILLIPS).

They Were Instructed to Be Sanctified Wholly
(I Thessalonians 5:23-24)

We have now bumped up against one of the key words in this matter of living a holy life—"sanctification." "It is God's will that you should be sanctified" Paul wrote in 4:3. The sanctification of the believer is one of the happy joys we experience in our relationship with the Lord.

What does the word "sanctification" mean?

"Sanctification" is an old and rich word.

In the Old Testament, the word was used to refer to any thing or any person who had been consecrated to God. Priests were sanctified to sacred service. Places, like the Temple, were sanctified for divine worship. The tools of worship were sanctified before they could be used. In the Old Testament, the word sanctification referred primarily to the act of giving something to God. This gift, with no strings attached, could be given by the individual believer or the believing community.

The New Testament made the word richer and fuller by keeping all the Old Testament meaning and adding a new dimension. That new dimension describes the act of God purifying or cleansing the gift. The Holy Spirit is the One who sanctifies the believing Christian and provides the strength to live a pure life.

Sanctified Christians can be blameless though not necessarily faultless. The distinction between blameless and faultless is far more than verbal aerobics.

"Blameless" comes from a word that means "to blaspheme." "Blasphemy is any act or word by which a person denies that God is God."[1] It is a willful act, a personal decision that replaces God on the throne of a person's life.

"Faultless" comes from a word that means "to disappoint." I can disappoint you because of the limitations of my humanness, my ignorance, and so forth, and not be held guilty for wrongdoing.

We're working toward an understanding of a proper definition of sin. "Sin is the [lack] of conformity to the divine law or standard of excellence. . . . In another sense, it is the willful transgression of a known law of God. This was John Wesley's definition of sin 'properly so-called.'"[2]

What happens when a person is sanctified? Paul promised that God would sanctify "through and through," identifying the fullness and completeness of the blessing. Hence the phrase "entire sanctification."

Sanctification includes the two crises of initial and entire sanctification. Initial sanctification takes place when a person is born again. Entire sanctification is a second crisis experience whereby the sinful nature is cleansed and the Christian is given the power to live a holy life.

When is a Christian sanctified?

It happens in a moment. The word "sanctify" in 5:23 identifies action that takes place in a moment, as contrasted with action taking place over a period of time. This is only one of several places in the New Testament that teach entire sanctification is a second work of divine grace following conversion.[3]

It takes a lifetime. The clear message of 4:3 and 4:7 is that the Christian is sanctified wholly to live a sanctified life. Entire sanctification makes an ever-expanding growth in Christian love possible (4:9).

To summarize, what have we learned from the Thessalonians about holy living?

- Every Christian is called to live a holy life.
- The sanctification of every believer is God's will.
- Sanctification takes both a moment and a lifetime.
- The God of peace is our sanctifier.

Because of the nature of humans, who could ever expect to make himself or herself holy? Nobody, that's who. But no one needs to do that. As Paul promised, "The one who calls you is faithful and he will do it" (5:24).

Praise His name!

Notes:

1. Albert Truesdale, et al., eds., *A Dictionary of the Bible and Christian Doctrine in Everyday English* (Kansas City: Beacon Hill Press of Kansas City, 1986), 43.

2. Richard S. Taylor, ed. *Beacon Dictionary of Theology* (Kansas City: Beacon Hill Press of Kansas City, 1983), 484.

3. For a fuller explanation and other scriptures, see Appendix, page 121.

Word to Remember: *May God himself, the God of peace, sanctify you through and through. May your whole spirit, soul and body be kept blameless at the coming of our Lord Jesus Christ* (1 Thessalonians 5:23).

Coming up . . . Christianity is optimistic. Men and women, girls and boys, are capable of unlimited improvement. That's the story of salvation history as recorded in the Holy Bible. Of course, it didn't look that way at the beginning of time. Nor does it always look that way for every individual. But it's true. Not in our strength, but in His.

In the previous chapter, we saw how victory in Christ can free us from sin and enable us to live above sin in this life. That spiritual experience is known as entire sanctification. In this chapter, we begin to discover some of the dimensions of a life lived with Christ as our Lord and Master. This Bible study is not the whole story, but it is part of what it means to live the Spirit-filled life.

Galatians 5:13-26

5 [13]You, my brothers, were called to be free. But do not use your freedom to indulge the sinful nature; rather, serve one another in love. [14]The entire law is summed up in a single command: "Love your neighbor as yourself." [15]If you keep on biting and devouring each other, watch out or you will be destroyed by each other.

[16]So I say, live by the Spirit, and you will not gratify the desires of the sinful nature. [17]For the sinful nature desires what is contrary to the Spirit, and the Spirit what is contrary to the sinful nature. They are in conflict with each other, so that you do not do what you want. [18]But if you are led by the Spirit, you are not under law.

[19]The acts of the sinful nature are obvious: sexual immorality, impurity and debauchery; [20]idolatry and witchcraft; hatred, discord, jealousy, fits of rage, selfish ambition, dissensions, factions [21]and envy; drunkenness, orgies, and the like. I warn you, as I did before, that those who live like this will not inherit the kingdom of God.

[22]But the fruit of the Spirit is love, joy, peace, patience, kindness, goodness, faithfulness, [23]gentleness and self-control. Against such things there is no law. [24]Those who belong to Christ Jesus have crucified the sinful nature with its passions and desires. [25]Since we live by the Spirit, let us keep in step with the Spirit. [26]Let us not become conceited, provoking and envying each other.

5

Live by the Spirit

NOT MANY people get angry about the color purple. In fact, if purple triggers a violent outburst, the family may want to give the troubled person a year's supply of visits to a qualified counselor.

However, if you paint purple stripes on the front of my gray-and-red brick home, you'll get my undivided attention. I've had some neighbors who, if treated that way, would inflict certain indignities on your body, making you a candidate for a large collection of "get well" cards on the wall of your hospital room.

Why the difference? A swatch of purple cloth lying on the counter does not attack my self-image, cause damage to my pocketbook, nor require a change in my behavior. Painted stripes do all this and more.

Perhaps that's why the Christian religion keeps causing trouble. Not because it is purple, but because it insists on being practical. It requires change in attitude and action.

That may be why the Holy Spirit has been so controversial across the centuries. To use an old and tired cliche, "This is where the rubber meets the road." The Holy Spirit is the member of the divine Trinity that puts all the beautiful truths into action. And because what He does puts pressure on us to change, Christians have long debated what those changes should be.

The best place we can go for an answer is the Holy Bible. This chapter takes us to one of the key passages in the letters of the apostle Paul on this subject. We will see what living the Spirit-filled life means.

A Responsible Use of Freedom
(Galatians 5:13-15)

I remember clearly the shouts of freedom that echoed through the openings that had been hastily punched in that ugly concrete barrier known as the Berlin Wall. Later, the sober realities of freedom gradually crept across Eastern Europe. People discovered once again that happy hilarity is neither the price nor the purpose of freedom. It is only an early by-product.

Many Bible scholars believe a similar situation existed in the churches of Galatia to which Paul wrote. The gospel of our Lord Jesus Christ had freed the Galatian Christians from the bondage of whatever gods they had worshiped. The apostle encouraged them to enjoy the full benefits of that freedom (5:1).

The temptation is to allow freedom to be the launching pad for self-indulgence (5:13). Paul repeats the same idea, using the same word as in Romans 7:8. The NASB helps us more here than the NIV when it translates Paul's phrase with these words, "Do not turn your freedom into an opportunity for the flesh" (5:13, emphasis added). The word "opportunity" was originally a military word for base of operations. It came to mean an excuse to do what you want to do.

The intense demands of self-indulgence are shown in 5:15 where the apostle uses the words "biting and devouring." Most of our cities have leash laws and animal-control officers. Rarely do we see animals running free; dangerous ones are quickly captured. In Paul's day, savage half-wild dogs ran unchecked through the cities, snapping at each other and gorging themselves on whatever they could find. Their only value came from the fact that they provided the city's only garbage removal, but at great cost to the safety of those who lived there. When freedom is abused for selfish purposes, this is the terrifying result.

The proper use of Christian freedom is to "serve one another in love" (5:13). We have now collided with an idea so common that, even though it is distinctly Christian, it has lost its raw power to change our behavior. The word "serve" means "be a slave to." However, we don't intend to be anybody's slave.

And yet . . .

The apostle declared this to be the essence of Christianity —to be slaves to one another in love. We walk with reverence here, for we are at the heart of the Christian faith. The Spirit-filled life is not holy hilarity, not financial success, but love and loving service. This is the responsible use of freedom.

A Rejection of the Flesh
(Galatians 5:16-21)

"All I know is just what I read in the papers," said the humorist Will Rogers.

You can discover what a community is like by reading the newspapers. It's true, of course, that every paper has an editorial position. Yet, editors are first of all merchants with a product to sell. If they don't print what interests their readers, eventually they'll be out of business. So, to some extent, you can find out what a community is like by reading the papers.

Do you want to know what Galatia was like? You can read it in the papers. Or, more specifically, you can read it in the words of the apostle Paul in Galatians 5:19-21.

Do the words seem harsh? They do to me. Yet, Paul was not nearly as pessimistic as the secular philosophers of his time. When we compare Paul with the moralists of his day, a fundamental difference jumps out. The pagans regarded the vices of their community with horror and concluded they were contrary to humanity's true nature. However, Paul says clearly that this is what you can expect when Christ is not honored as Lord.

Let's begin with something that sounds boring but is absolutely vital—definitions. The NIV uses the phrase "sinful nature" to translate the Greek word that literally means "flesh." The Greek word for "flesh" has a variety of meanings. Here, it clearly shows human nature dominated by sin—the sin principle, not just sins committed. (See Chapter 1 for a more complete discussion of this important distinction.) Flesh refers not to the human body, its bones and blood vessels, but to the person who has chosen to be dominated by sin rather than to walk in the Spirit.

The relationship between the flesh and the Spirit is not "cold war" but active conflict (5:17). Nor is this simply a war of words. As humans, we are not only participants in the battle, we are the battlefield. "These [flesh and Spirit] are in opposition to one another, so that *you* may not do the things that you please" (5:17, NASB, emphasis added). Paul was saying to the Galatian Christians, "You cannot live a Christian life while the flesh is in control." That is because the flesh will not be subject to the Lord but will use every opportunity to destroy what is good and holy. At this point, we should be warned that the flesh expresses itself not only in vicious actions but also in nasty attitudes (5:19-21).

Those who reject responsible freedom and indulge in sinful living "will not inherit the kingdom of God" (5:21). You can't get into heaven by doing the "right thing," that is by good works. But you can be kept out by doing what the flesh prompts you to do. At the core, however, we are not looking at "bad works" but at a willful decision to spurn Jesus as Lord.

We have come then to see that Christian freedom, freedom in the Spirit, is the basis for Christian ethics. The liberating work of Christ becomes the foundation on which the Christian life is built.

A Receptivity to Growth in the Spirit
(Galatians 5:22-26)

Walking in the Spirit begins with the crucified life. The crucified life is a drastic rejection of the devil and all his schemes, coupled with a happy acceptance of Christ's will, along with a willingness to allow our Lord to remake us in His image.

Earlier Paul testified to the Galatians, "I have been crucified with Christ and I no longer live, but Christ lives in me. The life I live in the body, I live by faith in the Son of God, who loved me and gave himself for me" (2:20). To the Romans he wrote, "If we have been united with him like this in his death, we will certainly also be united with him in his resurrection. For we know that our old self was crucified with him so that the body of sin might be done away with, that we should no longer be slaves to sin—because anyone who has died has been freed from sin" (6:5-7).

The crucified life is not "on hold." Anyone who has ever called a complaint department has heard the words, "Would you hold, please?" All VCR owners also know what it means to put the action on "pause." Paul strongly contends that vital Christian living is not static, not temporarily suspended from action.

Throughout this Galatians passage, the apostle keeps reminding us of the dynamic nature of vital Christianity. (See 5:16, 5:18, and 5:25 as examples.) One English word "walk" is used to translate two different Greek words in verses 16 and 25 in the NASB. In verse 16 the idea of the Greek word is that of habitual conduct. In verse 25, a military term is used, to march in battle order or to fall into line. That leads J. B. Phillips to these helpful translations: "Live your whole life in the Spirit" (v. 16). "Let us be guided by the Spirit" (v. 25).

Christians who are willing to trust themselves to the Holy Spirit will find that growing as a believer is not like going on a diet to gain weight, forcing oneself to eat even when not hungry. Rather, a simple openness to God's power and a commitment to follow where He leads will unlock new avenues of joy and blessing. Growing as a Christian is to be a natural expression of our life in the Lord.

Walking in the Spirit produces the fruit of the Spirit (5:22-23). Many Bible scholars have pointed out the contrast between the plural "deeds of the flesh" (NASB) or "acts of the sinful nature" (NIV) in verse 19 and the singular "fruit of the Spirit" (NIV and NASB) in verse 22. Sin tears life apart; the gospel builds life around a divine center.

What a joy to realize that the fruit of the Spirit is not like the gifts of the Spirit. Christians are given different gifts for the building of the Kingdom (Romans 12:6-8, for example). However, the fruit of the Spirit—*all* the fruit of the Spirit—is available for every Christian. Not everyone will be a preacher or a teacher, but all can grow in all aspects of the Spirit-filled life as described in verses 22-23.

What a happy privilege!

Word to Remember: *Those who belong to Christ Jesus have crucified the sinful nature with its passions and desires. Since we live by the Spirit, let us keep in step with the Spirit* (Galatians 5:24-25).

Coming up . . . Our goal in this series of Bible studies is to explore what it means to live a holy life. That search has taken us from the original sin in the garden to a lonely hill called Calvary and an empty tomb, which could not hold our Lord. We have rejoiced in the victory that is ours in Christ. Along the way, we have discovered that the Christian life is neither like a scientific experiment nor a mathematical formula. It is alive, dynamic, and changing because it is personal and intertwined with human experience.

In the previous chapter, we saw how the internal battle can be won. In the present chapter, we will explore what that victory means to our relationship with God and the people around us.

2 Corinthians 5:16-21

5 [16]So from now on we regard no one from a worldly point of view. Though we once regarded Christ in this way, we do so no longer. [17]Therefore, if anyone is in Christ, he is a new creation; the old has gone, the new has come! [18]All this is from God, who reconciled us to himself through Christ and gave us the ministry of reconciliation: [19]that God was reconciling the world to himself in Christ, not counting men's sins against them. And he has committed to us the message of reconciliation. [20]We are therefore Christ's ambassadors, as though God were making his appeal through us. We implore you on Christ's behalf: Be reconciled to God. [21]God made him who had no sin to be sin for us, so that in him we might become the righteousness of God.

2 Corinthians 6:14—7:1

6 [14]Do not be yoked together with unbelievers. For what do righteousness and wickedness have in common? Or what fellowship can light have with darkness? [15]What harmony is there between Christ and Belial? What does a believer have in common with an unbeliever? [16]What agreement is there between the temple of God and idols? For we are the temple of the living God. As God has said: "I will live with them and walk among them, and I will be their God, and they will be my people." [17]"Therefore come out from them and be separate, says the Lord. Touch no unclean thing, and I will receive you." [18]"I will be a Father to you, and you will be my sons and daughters, says the Lord Almighty."

7 [1]Since we have these promises, dear friends, let us purify ourselves from everything that contaminates body and spirit, perfecting holiness out of reverence for God.

6

The God Who Interrupts

THE 19TH-CENTURY British poet Arthur Hugh Clough wrote,

> *This world is very odd we see,*
> *We can't comprehend it;*
> *But in one fact we all agree,*
> *God won't, and we can't, mend it.*[1]

Is it any wonder the *Encyclopedia Britannica* observes that Clough's skepticism reflects the mood of the current century more than his own?

Nevertheless, cynicism does not share the same birth date as Clough. Long before Christ, the writer of Ecclesiastes said, "What has been will be again, what has been done will be done again; there is nothing new under the sun" (1:9).

Once a man named Saul, from the city of Tarsus, might have believed all that. He vigorously persecuted any who left the ancient faith to follow a prophet from Nazareth.

Then one day Saul's well-ordered world came crashing down around him. His conversion was so unexpected it made his former colleagues violently angry and his new friends understandably suspicious. Some of the implications of that change make up the core of this chapter's study.

We go to a passage in 2 Corinthians just following the apostle's defense of his ministry. There he gives us a clue about what motivated him, what should move us, and some additional hints on what it means to live a holy life.

God, the Aggressor
(2 Corinthians 5:18-21)

"If it's not broke, don't fix it," people tell us.
But we know it's "broke."

Sin broke it in the garden. And, as sinners, we kept breaking it. The original happy relationship with God the Father has been smashed to pieces. No wonder Paul could accurately say, "All have sinned and fall short of the glory of God" (Romans 3:23).

Do you react negatively to the phrase, "God, the aggressor"? I do. Then why use it? As the writer, I can describe God some other way. And many of those descriptions would be fitting and accurate.

Let's see how the word "aggressor" fits God. Aggression, says the dictionary, is an offensive action against an unfriendly nation. We said in the previous chapter that the relationship between the flesh and the Spirit is not "cold war" but active conflict. "[The flesh and Spirit] are in opposition to one another" (Galatians 5:17, NASB). As humans, we not only are participants in the battle but also are the battlefield.

It is a battle we cannot win. We cannot resolve our conflict with God by simply saying, "I have decided to be a friend of God. He will no longer be my enemy." Paul wrote to his Roman friends, "I am of flesh, sold into bondage to sin . . . I am not practicing what I would like to do, but I am doing the very thing I hate" (Romans 7:14-15, NASB). And that's not all. In the same way God placed a flaming sword to keep Adam and Eve out of the garden, we are banished from His presence, because, as sinners, we are God's enemies.

"God made [Jesus] who had no sin to be sin for us, so that in him we might become the righteousness of God" (2 Corinthians 5:21). Here is the gospel in all its majesty and mystery. Here is the distinctive message of Christianity. God reaching out to humanity, taking the initiative, being the "aggressor" against sin. This is not a priest standing at the altar, holding the still-beating heart of a human sacrifice aloft to the heavens, hoping to appease an angry God. Here is a loving God reaching down to take the hand of soiled and sinful men and women and lift them to himself. All this is God's gift to sinners.

One author has written, "Christians have [not] been given new ideals to live by [nor will they] experience a slow moral change brought about by a new desire to be good. They would then be recreating themselves. It is God who makes the new creation as He made the first, and as, according to Genesis, the first was not a gradual process neither is the second."[2] No wonder another writer said, "The Gospel is not good advice, but good news."[3]

Reconciliation, the Answer
(2 Corinthians 5:16-17; 6:14-18)

A chill swept through the small Christian community in Jerusalem. You don't have to know much history to understand why.

"Saul's back in town!" The word spread like wildfire.

"And what's more, he says he's a Christian and wants to know where we meet so he can join us. But I don't trust him."

"Neither do I!"

That might have been the end of it, except for Barnabas. Barnabas certified Saul's conversion (Acts 9:26-27). All that and more was in the apostle Paul's mind when he wrote, "So from now on we regard no one from a worldly point of view. Though we once regarded Christ in this way, we do so no longer" (2 Corinthians 5:16).

When we become Christians, we see people differently. When Paul writes about "a worldly point of view," he is not talking about the limitations that come from being human. He isn't saying, "If you knew him or her better, you'd understand." "Human judgments are not merely inadequate. They are also tinged with prejudice and bias. We make them with our own interests in mind."[4] We see people differently after we come to know Christ as Savior because we have a different point of view.

Our point of view has changed because we have been changed. It is not because we have decided to move so we can get a better view. Paul declared, "All this is from God, who reconciled us to himself through Christ" (5:18).

Reconciled!

That's not one of the most familiar words in the Christian vocabulary, but it ought to be. We speak more often of love and faith and hope. But it all began with reconciliation. The gospel message is summarized in these moving words, "God was reconciling the world to himself in Christ, not counting men's sins against them" (5:19).

Reconciled. Living the holy life is based on all that is wrapped up in this word. Thus, it will help us to ponder for a bit on what the word "reconciliation" means.

As with many other English words, the word "reconciliation" has become a bit fuzzy. We reconcile our checkbook, or try to, when we get our bank statement. Used that way, it means to balance accounts. We reconcile the various eyewitness reports of an accident by trying to discover what actually happened. We get two disputing parties to agree to a compromise and call it reconciliation. We accept a hardship we don't like by saying we've become reconciled to it. But none of these come close to what Paul meant when he talked about reconciliation.

Sometimes it is easier to illustrate than define. Ernest Best opens a window with these words,

> We come closer to what Paul is saying when we recall those human situations in which two people disagree, but one, though annoyed by the other, refuses to retaliate and seeks by word and action to win the other over. It happens sometimes when the child of a first marriage resents the arrival of a new marriage partner, but the new spouse seeks to gain the child with loving concern. So, God seeks to win us, and He shows His loving concern in the life and death of His Son.[5]

Put simply, the apostle meant, "We can't, but God will mend it."

Reconciliation provides both an opportunity and a challenge for holy living. We've examined the opportunity, now let's look at the challenge as defined by Paul in 2 Corinthians 6:14-18. One of the problems the new believers faced in the pagan city of Corinth was how "Christian" to be. The question captures our attention because we who would follow Christ face different but just as difficult issues.

There are no easy answers. No doubt we will always struggle to find a proper balance. On the one hand are the words of the prophet Isaiah, repeated by Paul, "Therefore come out from them and be separate, says the Lord" (6:17). And on the other, Paul commented on a popular idea of the day when he said, "'Everything is permissible'—but not everything is beneficial" (1 Corinthians 10:23). If we wander too far one way or the other, either complete separateness or "anything goes," we will lose our influence as His ambassadors.

We, the Ambassadors
(2 Corinthians 5:18b, 19b-20; 7:1)

Recently, the media carried the story of the appointment of a new ambassador to a troubled Central American country. Both critics and supporters of the government applauded the choice, saying, "He is a highly-qualified, career diplomat who knows both the language and the culture of the country to which he is going." Their applause was also a backhanded slap at the political cronies who are appointed to represent our country as ambassadors because of their supporting roles in national elections. Instinctively, we understand ambassadors should know more than how to win votes.

God, through Christ, has given us [the reconciled] the ministry and message of reconciliation. Our ministry is based on the fact that "in Christ" a person "is a new creation" (5:17), to which Paul adds, "All this is from God" (5:18).

The message of reconciliation rests on three truths:
- What Christ has done.
- What Christ has done for me.
- What Christ has done for me, He can also do for you.

"We are therefore Christ's ambassadors, as though God were making his appeal through us. We implore you on Christ's behalf: Be reconciled to God" (5:20). "Therefore, if anyone is in Christ, he is a new creation" (5:17). Only as Christ's new creation can we qualify as ambassadors for Christ. Because we are His new creation, we are His ambassadors. Not we *can* be, or *should* be, or *might* be. We *are!*

We are Christ's ambassadors—whether or not we want to be. We know enough about world politics to know there are good ambassadors and poor ones. What a humbling thought to realize He will be evaluated by others by the way we live.

What a joy to know that we have been given "the message of reconciliation" (5:19). What a responsibility. It begins, says Paul, with careful and constant attention to our personal spiritual journey. He writes, "Let us purify ourselves from everything that contaminates body and spirit, perfecting holiness out of reverence for God" (7:1). The emphasis is on both a decisive break with sin and sinning and a commitment to walk daily with our Lord. It happens in a moment and takes a lifetime. Because we are changed, and are being changed, we can be effective as His ambassadors.

Notes:

1. John Barlett, *Familiar Quotations,* 13th ed. (Boston: Little, Brown, and Company, 1955), 519.

2. Ernest Best, *Second Corinthians,* in *Interpretation* (Atlanta: John Knox Press, 1987), 54.

3. James Denny in *The International Bible Commentary,* F. F. Bruce, ed. (Grand Rapids: Zondervan Publishing House, 1986), 1399.

4. R. V. G. Tasker, *2 Corinthians,* vol. 8 of *Tyndale New Testament Commentaries* (Leicester, Eng.: InterVarsity Press, 1983), 53.

5. Best, *Interpretation,* 55-6.

Word to Remember: *Since we have these promises, dear friends, let us purify ourselves from everything that contaminates body and spirit, perfecting holiness out of reverence for God* (2 Corinthians 7:1).

Coming up . . . This series of Bible studies on living the holy life has combined two key elements: the grace of God and our freedom to respond to the divine call any way we choose. We experience God's saving power when we respond "yes" to His call upon our lives. We experience God's sanctifying power when we say "yes" to His way for our lives. Holy living has a definite instant of beginning. However, it is more than a moment caught in time. It is a day-by-day walk with the Lord.

Sometime during the second half of the first Christian century, a concerned pastor of a group of Jewish Christians wrote a letter to a congregation. That letter has been kept for us as the Book of Hebrews. Much of the letter is difficult for 21st-century Christians to understand. Nevertheless, the passage that this chapter explores is very up-to-date. How do we respond when things don't go well, especially when the uncomfortable or negative experiences appear to be God's way of guiding us? In other words, how should we react to God's discipline?

That's the focus of this chapter as we continue to explore how a hunger for God leads to holy living.

Hebrews 11:39—12:14

11 [39]These were all commended for their faith, yet none of them received what had been promised. [40]God had planned something better for us so that only together with us would they be made perfect.

12 [1]Therefore, since we are surrounded by such a great cloud of witnesses, let us throw off everything that hinders and the sin that so easily entangles, and let us run with perseverance the race marked out for us. [2]Let us fix our eyes on Jesus, the author and perfecter of our faith, who for the joy set before him endured the cross, scorning its shame, and sat down at the right hand of the throne of God. [3]Consider him who endured such opposition from sinful men, so that you will not grow weary and lose heart.

[4]In your struggle against sin, you have not yet resisted to the point of shedding your blood. [5]And you have forgotten that word of encouragement that addresses you as sons: "My son, do not make light of the Lord's discipline, and do not lose heart when he rebukes you, [6]because the Lord disciplines those he loves, and he punishes everyone he accepts as a son."

[7]Endure hardship as discipline; God is treating you as sons. For what son is not disciplined by his father? [8]If you are not disciplined (and everyone undergoes discipline), then you are illegitimate children and not true sons. [9]Moreover, we have all had human fathers who disciplined us and we respected them for it. How much more should we submit to the Father of our spirits and live! [10]Our fathers disciplined us for a little while as they thought best; but God disciplines us for our good, that we may share in his holiness. [11]No discipline seems pleasant at the time, but painful. Later on, however, it produces a harvest of righteousness and peace for those who have been trained by it.

[12]Therefore, strengthen your feeble arms and weak knees. [13]"Make level paths for your feet," so that the lame may not be disabled, but rather healed.

[14]Make every effort to live in peace with all men and to be holy; without holiness no one will see the Lord.

7

Discipline in the Holy Life

THE BOOK OF HEBREWS almost didn't get into the Bible. Looking back, this appears odd, especially since Hebrews is the most doctrinal book in the New Testament, next to Romans, and tells us more about Christ than any other part of the New Testament, except the Gospels.

The biggest questions swirled around the issue of authorship. This mystery was viewed differently in the eastern and western churches.

Hebrews was accepted as God's Word by the Eastern Church (generally the churches centered around Asia Minor) much earlier than the Western Church (which ultimately centered in Rome). Probably the Eastern Church accepted Hebrews because it concluded that the apostle Paul was the author.

In the West, most scholars decided Paul did not write Hebrews but could not agree on who did. As we know, Hebrews became a part of the Bible, though the question of authorship has never been settled.

If you read Hebrews 11:39—12:1 from some second-century manuscripts, it would look something like this:

GODHADPLANNEDSOMETHINGBETTERFORUS SOTHATONLYTOGETHERWITHUSWOULDTHEYBE MADEPERFECTTHEREFORESINCEWEARESURROUND EDBYSUCHAGREATCLOUDOFWITNESSES . . .

Except it would have been in Greek instead of English. All the letters would have been capitals. There would have been no separation between words and no division into verses and chapters.

Professor Stephen Langton of the University of Paris divided the Bible into the chapter divisions we still use. He

died in 1228. In 1551, a Paris printer named Robert Ste-
phens produced a Greek New Testament with verse divisions. The Old Testament, divided into chapters and verses,
followed in 1555. The first English translation divided in
this manner was the Geneva Bible of 1560.

The "invention" of chapters and verses has been a great
help to Bible study. It would be too confusing, but sometimes
I'd like to change the way these gentlemen divided the Bible.
This is one of those times, as our study will uncover later.

There are also times when, at least for study purposes, it
helps to "back into" the Bible passage. This would seem to
be one of those times as well. So, with that in mind, let's get
started.

The Dimensions of Holy Living
(Hebrews 12:12-14)

The Book of Hebrews is different from some pastoral
letters we've read. It is not an announcement of a special
speaker, nor a plea for money to pay off the loan on the new
furnace. Both are legitimate messages from a pastor to a
congregation. Instead, this pastoral letter is a call for Christians to accept the privileges and responsibilities of the faith
and not return to the old ways.

The opening line of verse 12 sounds like a sentence of
advice from a medical journal. "Strengthen your feeble arms
and weak knees." While the writer may have the imagery of
the sports arena from 12:1 in mind, the message is spiritual,
not physical. Feeble arms and weak knees describe tired
folks. Spiritually exhausted people ready to give up. We all
know the feeling. We also know how much easier it is to
quit when we are weary.

"Make straight paths for your feet" (12:13, NASB).
"Straight paths" is a more literal translation than "level
paths" in NIV. Used only here in the New Testament, the
word means, "path of a wheel." Yet, by implication, it can
mean smooth or level.

Straight paths are compared with natural paths that wind around rocks and trees, taking the way of least resistance. The straight, smooth road is one that has been prepared with some effort, "so that the lame may not be disabled" (12:13). What a vivid picture—a lame person's leg being dislocated because of the lack of careful preparation. As Christians, we have an obligation, not only for our own spiritual growth, but also to smooth and straighten the way for those weaker in the faith.

"Make every effort to live in peace with [everyone]" (12:14). These words catch the full force of the Greek. Being at peace with everyone is something to which we are to give our attention and energy in great degree. The temptation is to explain this away rather than work at it.

"Peace" is a great biblical word. It combines the Old Testament message of health and wholeness (shalom) with the New Testament idea of right relationship between God and us, as well as between those of us who crowd this planet. It has been called "the sense of restful well-being that comes from such right relationships."[1]

And we are admonished to "be holy," to which the pastor adds, "without holiness no one will see the Lord" (12:14). The proclamation, which concludes our study of 12:12-14, is a call to the sanctified life. A life dedicated to Jesus, cleansed by His Spirit, and active in taking the gospel to the world. This challenge is so far beyond us we are forced to ask, "How can this be done?" The pastor answers our question.

The Discipline That Is Required
(Hebrews 12:5-11)

Earlier in this book, we saw how divine power and human decision combined to enable believers to enter the sanctified life. In this chapter's study, we focus on one of the key elements in living the holy life—discipline.

Everything is going to be muddied unless we get a fairly

clear idea what the writer means by discipline. It quickly becomes obvious that we can ask more questions of these verses than they can answer. For example: How can we tell the difference between God's discipline, tough times, the devil at work, and our own dumb choices? Hebrews doesn't help us.

But all is not lost.

We do not have a word in English that has the same meaning as the Greek word used here. That's why the word is translated many different ways. Here are a few: encouragement, discipline, chastening, training, and correction. The word in the original is an old word referring to the whole process of training a child, including instruction, encouragement, correction, and punishment. In Ephesians 6:4, Paul used the same word to advise fathers to bring up their children in "the training and instruction of the Lord."

With that understanding of what the writer means, let's look at what he says about discipline.

Discipline is a demonstration of God's love. To the immature this sounds like a parent saying to a child about to be punished, "This hurts me more than it hurts you." Discipline and love seem to be opposites. "Why hurt the one you love?" we ask. The passing of the years changes our understanding until we finally learn that love sometimes causes some frustration or pain to save the loved one from greater agony. God is no different.

Discipline is a confirmation that we are members of God's family. Once again the line of reasoning has some very human overtones to it. "A father who neglects to discipline a son," writes one scholar, "is deficient in his capacity as a father, and a son who escapes all discipline is losing out on his sonship."[2] In fact, the writer to the Hebrews calls such persons "illegitimate children" (12:8). This is an especially tough concept for young parents in our day, where self-interest and short-term goals pay off so handsomely. Discipline requires the long look by a selfless person.

Discipline is intended to improve the one being disciplined.

Note the contrast: "Our fathers disciplined us for a little while as they thought best; but *God disciplines us for our good, that we may share in his holiness*" (12:10, emphasis added). As Christian believers, we are disciplined by a loving God, not for His self-interest nor to decrease His discomfort, but that we may share His holiness. The holy life is the disciplined life. Holy living submits to God's discipline and exercises self-discipline, as will become clear as we look at 12:1-4. (Remember that we are "backing into" this study.)

The Dynamic That Makes It Possible
(Hebrews 11:39—12:14)

We have now backed up to the point where Stephen Langton's chapter divisions hinder more than help. The 11th chapter of Hebrews is foundational to this section, especially verses 39-40.

The decision to "back into" this study has also highlighted one of the problems people face with holy living. Too often the holy life has been described as a list of things to be done or avoided. The "shoulds" and "should nots" of life. Of course, these are part of the sanctified life. However, when a period is put at the end of the list, we almost insure that people will be frustrated. No one can live the holy life without divine help and the awareness that holy living is not identical with keeping lists—even good lists.

Holy living is far more than keeping lists by gritting our teeth and clenching our fists in determination to be successful. We begin by recognizing we are not alone.

"Since we are surrounded by such a great cloud of witnesses" (12:1). What witnesses? All the heroes of chapter 11, as well as all they represent and anticipate. The word translated "witness" is the Greek word for "martyr." It tells us something of the character of those who view from the stands in this symbolism taken from the Greek Olympic games.

The Hebrew view of history must also be a part of our

understanding of this picture. The Jews believed the past was a part of the present. The Hebrews preacher and his congregation, then, would have no difficulty thinking of the saints of the past sharing in the event taking place in the present. They were not just dead heroes who inspired; their spirits were alive and active in the fulfillment of their hopes and dreams.

The writer of Hebrews challenges us to action in 12:1. Just what is it that we are summoned to do?

- "Throw off everything that hinders."

Bible scholars see this as including all that was involved in preparation for the Greek Olympic games—everything from vigorous training, which strengthened the body and reduced unnecessary fat, to the robe that was discarded just before the race because it would hinder the athlete as he ran. The Christian is to discard everything, both good and bad, that makes living a holy life more difficult.

- "And the sin that so easily entangles."

No doubt the writer deliberately chose not to identify a list of sins here. Maybe, for two reasons: First, the "entangling" sin is not the same for every Christian. Not everyone is vulnerable to the same temptations. Second, and more important, the issue is sin, not merely sins. Who we are, how we think, what attitudes we hold—not just what we do. It is not some particular sin that causes trouble. Sin itself is the problem.

- "Run with perseverance."

Our generation, which demands immediate gratification for every desire, needs this encouragement as much as any generation in history.

In verse 3, the Hebrews writer advises, "Consider [Jesus]." We have now come to the power room for holy living. The choice to use the human name, Jesus, is significant. Earlier, we were challenged to "fix our eyes on Jesus" (12:2). Jesus is the knowable God. Jesus is God in human form, tempted in every way as we are, yet without sin. The man Jesus provides the possibility and the power for living the holy life. He makes it possible for us to live the holy life without growing weary and losing heart.

Conclusion

Now we have backed our way to the beginning. Now we see that holy living requires effort on our part. Strengthening feeble arms and weak knees. Making every effort to live peaceable lives. And it means accepting discipline from the Lord, as it shows how much He loves us as our Heavenly Father. And finally, it means looking at the perfect example of Jesus, how He lived His life in sacrifice for us.

All of this together enables us to persevere in our faith until we reach those heavenly shores, where we can speak face-to-face with the "great cloud of witnesses," and join them in worshiping God forevermore.

Notes:

1. W. T. Purkiser, *Hebrews, James, Peter,* vol. 11 of *Beacon Bible Expositions* (Kansas City: Beacon Hill Press of Kansas City, 1974), 108.

2. Donald Guthrie, *Hebrews,* vol. 15 of *Tyndale New Testament Commentaries* (Grand Rapids: William B. Eerdmans Publishing Company, 1983), 253.

Word to Remember: *Endure hardship as discipline; God is treating you as sons. For what son is not disciplined by his father?* (Hebrews 12:7).

Coming up . . . In the mosaic we have been building, called "a holy life," we looked in the previous chapter at discipline—God's discipline of the devout. We learned that God's discipline requires the believer to exercise self-discipline in response.

We live in a day that honors self-discipline, at least some forms of it. We give special recognition to those who stay on their diets and maintain exercise programs. Lean bodies and flat stomachs are among the gods our culture worships.

The present chapter reminds us that holy living is more than style, more than self-discipline. History records that some of the most destructive people have been the most disciplined. Isaiah will help us see that conduct flows from character, that the disciplined life does not please God when self-interest is king.

Isaiah 58:1-12

12 ¹"Shout it aloud, do not hold back.
    Raise your voice like a trumpet.
Declare to my people their rebellion
    and to the house of Jacob their sins.
²For day after day they seek me out;
    they seem eager to know my ways,
as if they were a nation that does what is right
    and has not forsaken the commands of its God.
They ask me for just decisions
    and seem eager for God to come near them.
³'Why have we fasted,' they say,
    'and you have not seen it?
Why have we humbled ourselves,
    and you have not noticed?'
"Yet on the day of your fasting, you do as you please
    and exploit all your workers.
⁴Your fasting ends in quarreling and strife,
    and in striking each other with wicked fists.
You cannot fast as you do today
    and expect your voice to be heard on high.
⁵Is this the kind of fast I have chosen,
    only a day for a man to humble himself?
Is it only for bowing one's head like a reed
    and for lying on sackcloth and ashes?
Is that what you call a fast,
    a day acceptable to the LORD?
⁶"Is not this the kind of fasting I have chosen:
    to loose the chains of injustice
    and untie the cords of the yoke,
to set the oppressed free
    and break every yoke?
⁷Is it not to share your food with the hungry
and to provide the poor wanderer with shelter—
when you see the naked, to clothe him,
    and not to turn away from your own flesh and blood?
⁸Then your light will break forth like the dawn,
    and your healing will quickly appear;
then your righteousness will go before you,

and the glory of the LORD will be your rear guard.
⁹Then you will call, and the LORD will answer;
    you will cry for help, and he will say: Here am I.
"If you do away with the yoke of oppression,
    with the pointing finger and malicious talk,
¹⁰and if you spend yourselves in behalf of the hungry
    and satisfy the needs of the oppressed,
then your light will rise in the darkness,
    and your night will become like the noonday.
¹¹The LORD will guide you always;
    he will satisfy your needs in a sun-scorched land
    and will strengthen your frame.
You will be like a well-watered garden,
    like a spring whose waters never fail.
¹²Your people will rebuild the ancient ruins
    and will raise up the age-old foundations;
you will be called Repairer of Broken Walls,
    Restorer of Streets with Dwellings.

8

Rebels That
Look Religious

WHAT WAS IT like in Judah after the Exile? This question speaks to a couple of things we have to deal with up front. Whatever date is set for the writing of the Book of Isaiah, there is pretty general agreement that the subject of chapter 58 is Judah after the people returned from Babylon.

Only the people from Judah, the Southern Kingdom, returned from exile. The Assyrians repopulated Samaria, the Northern Kingdom, after it fell in 722 B.C. The exiles from those tribes became a part of the culture where they were taken.

Only the poorest were allowed to remain as caretakers of Judah. The exiles returned to poverty and a depressed economy. Money was hard to come by. Many scholars feel that Haggai 2:1-3 indicates that the older people were discouraged when they saw the financial problems. The Temple under construction was plain when compared to the magnificent structure Solomon had built.

Such was the situation that Isaiah, the famous biblical prophet, dealt with in the later chapters of the book that bears his name as he brought God's message to the people. A biblical prophet was, first of all, a preacher. He or she might not be an "ordained elder," to use our modern term. Prophets usually did not have ecclesiastical credentials, nor did they enjoy the approval of "organized religion."

The Lord ordained the prophets, sending them out to deliver His message because "organized religion" had become sidetracked. Prophets spoke for God. In fact, their primary task was forthtelling. Sometimes that *forth*telling included predictions about the future, that is, *fore*telling.

This chapter's exploration is based on the confidence that the Lord informed the foreteller and gave courage to the forthteller. My Sunday School teacher these days, keeps reminding us that we have the Bible, and each part of it, because the Holy Spirit prompted the Church to keep it. Part of our task in Bible study is to discover what the Holy Spirit wants us to learn from each passage.

If this is true, as I believe it is, then our most important task in this Old Testament Bible study is not to argue whether the prophet was foretelling or forthtelling, but to determine what the Lord has in it for us. That will be our approach as we study Isaiah 58:1-12.

Rebels That Look Religious
(Isaiah 58:1-5)

Terrorism used to have a recognizable face, but not any more. A plane crashes into a quiet town because some unidentified person put a bomb on board. People die because a nondescript truck filled with dynamite explodes by remote control. Unknown hijackers fly jumbo jets into giant buildings and kill thousands of innocent persons. It's true, of course, that many times when the terrorists are captured, they look fierce and dangerous. However, that wasn't the case in Isaiah's time.

The rebels Isaiah wrote about looked religious. Keep in mind that it is the great God of salvation-history who speaks in the Bible passage under consideration here. Through His prophet, the Lord said these remarkable things about the people:

- Day after day they seek Him out.
- They seem eager to know His ways.
- They ask Him for just decisions.
- They seem eager for God to come near them.

Isaiah was not preaching to a bunch of tough hombres

in a western saloon. These were good people—fine, up-standing, religious. The "holy" people of their day.

But God said, "Raise your voice like a trumpet. Declare to my people their rebellion" (58:1). What was the nature of their rebellion? "Rebellion is," one writer explains, "doing one's own pleasure or as one wishes in worship . . . rather than as God wishes."[1] That insistent, though not necessarily belligerent, mood did not disappear in the mists of ancient history. The theme song of our permissive age may well be the tune popular many years back, "I Did It My Way."

The Lord called these people bad, not because they were aggressively evil, but because they were consumed by self-interest.

Because of their selfish attitudes and actions, they learned that religious forms can be empty.

It will help us to recall life in Jerusalem at the time about which Isaiah prophesied. What was it like in Jerusalem after the Exile? Actually, life was pretty grim. A few unimpressive stone huts built from the debris of the city destroyed years earlier. The Temple? Gone! The walls? Flattened! The economy? In shambles!

Controlled by foreign governments, watched by alien troops, the people began to rebuild. As is always the case, some people made money and built fine homes while the majority was poor and homeless. It appears that it was the members of the upper class who complained to God, and to whom God directed His scathing words.

"Why have we fasted," they say, "and you have not seen it?" (58:3). What they meant by this question was, "Look around Lord. What do You see? This place is a mess. We didn't know it was going to be this tough when we left Babylon. We've been doing all the religious things, fasting and the like. Where have You been? Why have we humbled ourselves, and You have not noticed?"

We get a clearer focus on this scene when we remember that "in the Semitic way of speaking, 'fasting' meant more than refraining from eating. The word stood for all that was implied in a self-righteous religiosity that divorced faith from love."[2] Theirs was a selfishness with a veneer of holiness, rebellion that looked like religion. At least on the surface.

But they didn't fool God.

Religion That Pleases God
(Isaiah 58:6-12)

The closing verses of this passage contain the music of joy. They express all the people wanted, and more. We don't have to analyze these verses to understand them. They are vibrant, alive, full of emotion. They speak of light, healing, God's presence, divine guidance, answered prayer, good health, unfailing strength, and final victory in their task of rebuilding the ruined city. They show that the Lord honors sincere worship.

Place yourself in the people's shoes, surrounded by the remnants of a conquering army's anger. Weep over the lost glory of the Holy City. Then hear the Lord say, "Your people will rebuild the ancient ruins and will raise up the age-old foundations; you will be called Repairer of Broken Walls, Restorer of Streets with Dwellings" (v. 12). If that doesn't bring tears of joy and shouts of victory, then you need to check your pulse—or check your remains into the care and keeping of the nearest funeral director. Nevertheless, before you do either, remember God's promises always come with an "if" attached.

Fasting became a major event in Israel following the Exile. In fact, there were four major fasts calling the people to remember the destruction of Jerusalem.

Fasting had long been a part of Hebrew worship. It was a way to express sorrow or distress over personal sin or national transgression. Never before this time, however, had fasting been a part of institutionalized religious worship. Fasts were an occasional, irregular event. Following the Exile, they were placed on the calendar and celebrated regularly.

The word "celebrated" is carefully chosen, for these fasts were not days of national mourning but feasts of joy. Actually, they were popular occasions that had little or nothing to do with worship.

Apparently this is what happened: a "holy day" became a "holiday." What had started out as a time of national remembrance for the sins of the past had become a grand opportunity to sin in the present.

Except they didn't consider themselves to be sinning, but God did. It is at this point that the ancient record has a vital message for anyone who would strive to live a holy life in our day. The Lord charged them with hypocrisy. Their actions did not match their testimony. Nor could their motives stand up under the unflinching scrutiny of a holy God.

The Lord described how a religious person, a holy person, should act. He did it by using the same symbol they had used to complain to Him—fasting. It's as if the Lord said, "Take a careful look at what you do, and why you do what you do on your fast days. Now, let Me tell you what I think a fast should be."

The prophecy is clear. The person who would lead a righteous life, a holy life, would redefine what worship meant and redirect his or her income and energies to help the less fortunate. After a scathing rebuke of their fast days in verse 5, God describes the life that pleases Him. This is the kind of fast the Lord chooses:

- "To loose the chains of injustice . . . to set the oppressed free and break every yoke" (58:6).

Earlier God said, "On the day of your fasting, you . . . exploit all your workers" (v. 3). Their religious devotion did not carry over to the world of business and interpersonal relationships.

Israel was still an occupied nation, a Persian colony. Nevertheless, God basically said, "The problem is not with others, not with the Persians. It is in your own hearts. You must break the bonds you use to keep other people down."

- "To share your food with the hungry and to provide the poor wanderer with shelter" and clothe the naked (58:7a).

The word "share" is powerful as used here. Literally, it means "to break in two." It carries this message: if you have a loaf, break it in half and give half to a hungry person. Bring the homeless into your home and let them live in half of it. Clothe the naked from your own wardrobe. And while you are at it, make sure they are dressed as well as you.

- "[Do] not . . . turn away from your own flesh and blood" (58:7b).

Strange isn't it, how much easier it is to deny kinship than to help our brothers and sisters in the Lord? "But that's Old Testament," you say. Before you get too comfortable, think on these words from Jesus:

> Then the righteous will answer him, "Lord, when did we see you hungry and feed you, or thirsty and give you something to drink? When did we see you a stranger and invite you in, or needing clothes and clothe you? When did we see you sick or in prison and go to visit you?" The King will reply, "I tell you the truth, *whatever you did for one of the least of these brothers of mine, you did for me*" (Matthew 25:37-40, emphasis added).

Conclusion

This word from God through the prophet Isaiah is challenging to us. Are we really rebels dressed up in religious trappings? Does our fasting please God or make a mockery of His intentions?

Hard questions. Our truthful answers reveal whether we truly hunger for God or accept a dissatisfying substitute for the holy life.

Notes:

1. John D. W. Watts, *Isaiah 34—66*, vol. 25 of *Word Biblical Commentary* (Waco, Tex.: Word Books, 1987), 273.

    2. George A. F. Knight, *The New Israel: Isaiah 56—66,* in *International Theological Commentary* (Grand Rapids: William B. Eerdmans Publishing Company, 1985), 22.

Word to Remember: *The King will reply, "I tell you the truth, whatever you did for one of the least of these brothers of mine, you did for me"* (Matthew 25:40).

Coming up . . . The problem with this chapter is that it's too predictable. When we started this series on living the holy life, we knew we were going to get here, sooner or later. Yet, that doesn't keep us from dreading being "beaten over the head" with something we know is a problem for everyone.

We've been told so often that our untamed tongues cause problems, we get bored almost to tears when the subject comes up again. And the truth is, there is probably nothing new in this Bible study.

Then why study it?

Because these words from James zero in on a problem we all face, and must have God's help to solve.

Of all the chapters in this series, this is one we must not dodge. Still, we will not despair. If we pay attention, we may uncover a new ray of hope by looking at a familiar subject.

James 3:1-12

3 [1]Not many of you should presume to be teachers, my brothers, because you know that we who teach will be judged more strictly. [2]We all stumble in many ways. If anyone is never at fault in what he says, he is a perfect man, able to keep his whole body in check.

[3]When we put bits into the mouths of horses to make them obey us, we can turn the whole animal. [4]Or take ships as an example. Although they are so large and are driven by strong winds, they are steered by a very small rudder wherever the pilot wants to go. [5]Likewise the tongue is a small part of the body, but it makes great boasts. Consider what a great forest is set on fire by a small spark. [6]The tongue also is a fire, a world of evil among the parts of the body. It corrupts the whole person, sets the whole course of his life on fire, and is itself set on fire by hell.

[7]All kinds of animals, birds, reptiles and creatures of the sea are being tamed and have been tamed by man, [8]but no man can tame the tongue. It is a restless evil, full of deadly poison.

[9]With the tongue we praise our Lord and Father, and with it we curse men, who have been made in God's likeness. [10]Out of the same mouth come praise and cursing. My brothers, this should not be. [11]Can both fresh water and salt water flow from the same spring? [12]My brothers, can a fig tree bear olives, or a grapevine bear figs? Neither can a salt spring produce fresh water.

Psalm 19:1-14

19 [1]The heavens declare the glory of God;
the skies proclaim the work of his hands.
[2]Day after day they pour forth speech;
night after night they display knowledge.
[3]There is no speech or language
where their voice is not heard.
[4]Their voice goes out into all the earth,
their words to the ends of the world.
In the heavens he has pitched a tent for the sun,
[5]which is like a bridegroom coming forth from his pavilion,
like a champion rejoicing to run his course.
[6]It rises at one end of the heavens

and makes its circuit to the other;
    nothing is hidden from its heat.
[7]The law of the LORD is perfect,
    reviving the soul.
The statutes of the LORD are trustworthy,
    making wise the simple.
[8]The precepts of the LORD are right,
    giving joy to the heart.
The commands of the LORD are radiant,
    giving light to the eyes.
[9]The fear of the LORD is pure,
    enduring forever.
The ordinances of the LORD are sure
    and altogether righteous.
[10]They are more precious than gold,
    than much pure gold;
they are sweeter than honey,
    than honey from the comb.
[11]By them is your servant warned;
    in keeping them there is great reward.
[12]Who can discern his errors?
    Forgive my hidden faults.
[13]Keep your servant also from willful sins;
    may they not rule over me.
Then will I be blameless,
    innocent of great transgression.
[14]May the words of my mouth and the meditation of my heart
    be pleasing in your sight,
        O LORD, my Rock and my Redeemer.

9

May My Words Please You, O God

THE SERIOUSNESS with which slander and gossip was regarded by ancient rabbis can be seen by the suggested punishment: "Whoever speaks slander is deserving to be stoned to death."

They recognized that without someone to listen it would be impossible to commit slander. And so they said, "The retailer of slander, the receiver of it, and he who gives false witness against his fellow, deserves to be cast to the dogs."

"There are four great sins," they also wrote. "They are idolatry, incest, murder, slander, the last of which is as bad as all the others put together." For the ancient Jew, no sin was taken more seriously than gossip and slander.

When we study what James had to say about the tongue, it is helpful to remember that he was writing to Jews who had been taught by the rabbis who quoted the above sayings.

We have sayings of our own. For example, "Sticks and stones can break my bones, but words will never hurt me!" Most of us, as children, used those words in defense when we were teased. Yet, we don't believe them any more now than we did then. Broken bones heal in a few weeks. A broken spirit, damaged by vicious words, sometimes doesn't heal in a lifetime.

Is there anyone among us who is not guilty? Anyone who has not used sharp words to hurt another person deliberately?

Probably not!

The only ones not guilty are those who are not "intelligent" enough to be mean, or "normal" enough to be held responsible for their words. That's why the rest of us need to pay close attention to these familiar words from James.

The Mother Tongue
(James 3:1-8, 10b-12)

A young Brazilian broke into tears at the airline ticket counter. He had been placed on the wrong plane in New York City. Consequently, no one met him when he got off the plane at Kansas City. He spoke no English. Nor could anyone speak Portuguese, his native language. Having never traveled outside Brazil, he was confused and a bit frightened.

Suddenly he heard the words, "Can I help?" Not in English. In Portuguese. A fellow Brazilian overheard him speak and stopped to listen. Since she could also speak English, she was able to unravel his problem quickly.

There are few sounds as sweet as those first heard at a mother's knee. Our mother tongue—the language we learned as a child—will never be replaced in our affection, no matter how many other languages we master. Wars have been fought, nations divided, people killed trying to decide the "right" language for a region.

There are thousands of languages and dialects in the world. James said there is one aspect common to all—the language of bitterness and hatred. This, wrote the brother of Jesus, is everyone's mother tongue. James used the tongue as a symbol of the disease to which no one is immune.

The tongue has great power. James used two illustrations his readers would have quickly understood. They comprised the two main forms of transportation in the first century, horses (or donkeys) and ships. Both illustrations deliver the same truth: something large controlled by something small. Horses have great power compared to humans. Yet, they can be controlled by a small metal bit in their mouth. Ancient ships were tiny compared to modern luxury liners or oil freighters. Yet, history records ancient ships that could carry a thousand passengers, all guided by a small rudder.

"Likewise the tongue is a small part of the body, but it makes great boasts" (3:5). The word "boast," as James used it, does not carry a negative message. J. B. Phillips' paraphrase captures the idea correctly, "The human tongue is physically small, but what tremendous effects it can boast of!"

The power of the tongue can be misused with disastrous results. Abruptly the mood changes. Using his pen like a sword, James quickly slashes away any illusions about the tongue. This is not a pretty section. Look what James says:

- "The tongue . . . is a fire" (v. 6).
- "It corrupts the whole person" (v. 6).
- "No man can tame the tongue" (v. 8).
- "It is a restless evil, full of deadly poison" (v. 8).
- "With the tongue we praise our Lord and Father, and with it we curse men, who have been made in God's likeness" (v. 9).

Since "out of the same mouth come praise and cursing," is it any wonder James said, "My brothers, this should not be" (v. 10)?

"With the tongue we . . . curse men, who have been made in God's likeness" (v. 9). This observation is a good example of the destructiveness of the tongue. When we use the word "curse," we mean profanity, but that's not how James used it.

In the first century, to curse a person was to express the hope that evil and tragedy would come to him or her. It was more like a witch's hex or a voodoo curse. "May your children become idolaters and your wife be unfaithful," was a commonly used curse in first-century Jerusalem.[1] No wonder James said that curses come straight from hell.

To curse someone in the first century was pretty serious business. Of course, curses of this kind are not common in the world you and I live in. Still, as one writer observes, "The spirit or attitude that produced it still exists and needs to be recognized as sin."[2]

There is one more truth we must look at before we rush from this "distasteful" section. If we are not careful, we will miss the key point of James's message. All these images—the bit in the horse's mouth, the rudder of a ship, our ability to tame wild animals—emphasize the idea of control. We can control horses, ships, and animals. But, ultimately, James's message is about destiny. *As the bit determines the direction the horse will go, and the rudder the ship, so our tongue can seal our destiny.*

That's a frightening thought. Especially when you recall James's words, "No man can tame the tongue" (3:8). We need help. Praise God, it's available!

The Father's Remedy
(James 3:9-10*a*)

Early television Westerns had several predictable story lines. One was about the gunslinger dying of thirst whose horse had run away. He crawls across the burning desert sand toward a freshwater spring. When he arrives, unable to go any further, he discovers to his horror that the spring's life-giving water has turned to alkali. He is condemned to die, the victim of fickle nature.

That, however, is not James's message here.

"With the tongue we [can] praise our Lord and Father" (3:9). The physical ability is not the issue, of course. Nor are examples lacking. History is filled with the sounds of praise. The Psalms are a hymnbook of praise (Psalms 19 and 23 are just two of many examples).

Praising God played a vital role in Hebrew worship. "The Holy One, Blessed be He," was one of the most frequent descriptions of God in rabbinical literature. The Eighteen Benedictions, a guide to worship used daily, concluded each section with a blessing to God. Christians picked up that theme. Recall the words of Paul to the Ephesians,

"Praise be to the God and Father of our Lord Jesus Christ, who has blessed us in the heavenly realms with every spiritual blessing in Christ" (1:3).

However, springs, fig trees, grapevines, and people all produce according to their nature. That is the awful tragedy of humanity. Our deceitful tongue is "a barometer of [our] spirituality."[3] Jesus spoke to this same issue. He said, "The things that come out of the mouth come from the heart, and these make a man 'unclean.' For out of the heart come evil thoughts, murder, adultery, sexual immorality, theft, false testimony, slander" (Matthew 15:18-19).

We sadly testify to the reality that we cannot control our sinful nature, we cannot "tame the tongue." The early Christian writer Augustine has a beautiful thought that helps us here. James "does not say that no one can tame the tongue, but no one of men; so that when it is tamed, we confess that this is brought about by the . . . grace of God."[4] Praise God for the divine power that can cleanse from sin and remake us so we can live daily in "the cleansing stream."[5] The Father's remedy for the polluted spring is to cleanse it and keep it clean.

A Child's Prayer
(Psalm 19:1-14)

"Two things fill the mind with ever new and increasing admiration and awe," said Immanuel Kant, "the starry heavens above and the moral law within."[6] Both of these are found in Psalm 19. The first part of the psalm, verses 1-6, is a hymn of praise to God as seen in nature. Verse 1 is an example of the devotional tone of this section: "The heavens declare the glory of God; the skies proclaim the work of his hands."

Both the mood and the style change at verse 7. This short section is reminiscent of Psalm 119 with its reverence for the law of God. The change is dramatically seen in the words used to identify God. In verse 1 God is El, the God of power. In contrast, seven times in verses 7-14 God is called

Yahweh (YAH-way). Yahweh is the personal God of the Hebrews, the God who brought them out of Egypt and into Canaan, the God of salvation-history.

The mood changes again at verse 13. Could it be that, as the psalmist looked at God in nature and God in His revealed Word, he saw his own unworthiness? Many a sincere worshiper has reacted this way. Isaiah, in the Temple, said, "Woe is me! For I am lost . . . for my eyes have seen the King, the Lord of hosts!" (6:5, RSV).

In the presence of the Almighty, the psalmist prayed that the Lord would help him live in such a way that his life would honor God: "Forgive my hidden faults. Keep your servant also from willful sins" (19:12-13).

As far as we know, no one in the Old Testament thought of the Almighty as Father. Jesus used the beautiful word "Abba," the Aramaic equivalent to the English word "Daddy," in Mark 14:36. However, the psalmist in the closing verses of Psalm 19 expresses a sense of intimacy not often found in the Old Testament. With the combination of humility and trust, he prayed a humble, childlike prayer: "May the words of my mouth and the meditation of my heart be pleasing in your sight, O LORD, my Rock and my Redeemer."

We could say no better words.

Notes:

1. *Hebrews—Revelation*, vol. 12 of *The Broadman Bible Commentary* (Nashville: Broadman Press, 1972), 124.

2. *Hebrews*, 124.

3. R. V. G. Tasker, *James*, vol. 16 of *Tyndale New Testament Commentaries* (Grand Rapids: William B. Eerdmans Publishing Co., 1983), 129.

4. Tasker, *James*, 127.

5. "The Cleansing Wave," *Sing to the Lord* (Kansas City: Lillenas Publishing Co., 1993), 520.

6. Tasker, *James*, 99.

Word to Remember: *May the words of my mouth and the meditation of my heart be pleasing in your sight, O LORD, my Rock and my Redeemer* (Psalm 19:14).

Coming up ... Holy living isn't getting any easier. Not if you judge it by what we've learned so far in these chapters. We started with original sin, which in a sense programs us to do bad things. And we perfect the art of doing bad things throughout the formative years of our lives. The good news is we encounter a saving, sanctifying Christ who can rewrite and debug our program. But then look what He demands of us after our reprogramming. We are to pursue spiritual growth. We are to help others. We are to control our criticisms. And if that's not hard enough, in this passage from Matthew we will see that He asks us to love our enemies. If you haven't figured it out yet, He is asking us to do what is humanly impossible. Fortunately, He doesn't abandon us to our human resources.

5 [38]"You have heard that it was said, 'Eye for eye, and tooth for tooth.' [39]But I tell you, Do not resist an evil person. If someone strikes you on the right cheek, turn to him the other also. [40]And if someone wants to sue you and take your tunic, let him have your cloak as well. [41]If someone forces you to go one mile, go with him two miles. [42]Give to the one who asks you, and do not turn away from the one who wants to borrow from you.

[43]"You have heard that it was said, 'Love your neighbor and hate your enemy.' [44]But I tell you: Love your enemies and pray for those who persecute you, [45]that you may be sons of your Father in heaven. He causes his sun to rise on the evil and the good, and sends rain on the righteous and the unrighteous. [46]If you love those who love you, what reward will you get? Are not even the tax collectors doing that? [47]And if you greet only your brothers, what are you doing more than others? Do not even pagans do that? [48]Be perfect, therefore, as your heavenly Father is perfect.

10

How to Love the Not-So-Lovely

THIS IS A dangerous chapter.

It's dangerous to write. It's dangerous to teach. It's dangerous to discuss. No matter what I write or what you say in your study session, we may all take flak from fellow Christians.

If we say Jesus literally meant we're to turn the other cheek, give up everything we have including the shirts off our backs, and love people who would kill us if they got the chance, we take flak. It comes from Christians who say Jesus would not ask us to do an impossible thing; He obviously had a deeper meaning in mind.

If we say He didn't literally mean what He said, we take flak. It comes from Christians who think we're watering down the teachings of Jesus, that we're trying to prove He didn't say what He very clearly said.

It's "friendly fire" in military lingo.

So even though this is a familiar passage and we may already have our minds made up, perhaps we could agree to set our opinions aside long enough to take a fresh look at the words of Jesus.

Bite Your Tongue, Not Your Neighbor
(Matthew 5:38-39)

In Jewish history, the law of an eye for an eye dates back to the time of Moses, perhaps 1,500 years before New Testament times. But this idea is older than Moses. It's at least as old as the Babylonian Code of Hammurabi.

Hammurabi was the last great king of the first Babylonian dynasty (approximately 1790—1750 B.C.). The Code of Hammurabi was a collection of laws safeguarding the rights and defining the responsibilities of Babylonian citizens. These laws, carved on stone pillars, were erected near temples and marketplaces. The best-preserved pillar containing the Code of Hammurabi is in the Louvre in Paris. It stands about seven feet high and is inscribed with about 250 laws.

The Code of Hammurabi is similar to collections of laws found among other ancient peoples, such as the Assyrians, Hittites, and the Hebrews. There are, however, some very important differences. Many Bible historians think the Babylonian ruler only recorded and edited laws that civilized people had been living by for centuries. Hammurabi's laws dealt with practical matters, whereas ethical and spiritual matters were of great importance to the Hebrews guided by the laws of God given through Moses.

This law of an "eye for an eye" didn't call for revenge. In fact, it limited revenge and pointed people toward justice. No longer was it legal to kill an entire family in retaliation for a single death, as tribal law allowed and sometimes encouraged.

Even today, retaliation is hard to control. Recently, I saw a videotape on a TV news program. One segment showed Israel's response after a 16-year-old Palestinian living near Bethlehem threw a fiery Molotov cocktail at an army patrol. No one was injured. The boy was arrested. His punishment, jail. The family's punishment, the demolition of their home. I watched as their small, one-story house exploded in a ball of fire that filled the screen. Rock fragments and splintered timber flew four times higher than the house had been, then rained back into a mound of rubble. The family moved into tents across the street.

One Israeli psychologist said he opposed this kind of harsh treatment. He said it breeds hatred between the two sides and hardens the soldiers, making them even more brutal.

In ancient days, and certainly in Christ's day, most people did not take literally the law of an eye for an eye. Financial damages replaced physical penalties. Consider this excerpt from Hammurabi's code: "If a man knocks out the tooth of a peasant, he shall pay one-third maneh of silver." A *maneh* weighed between one and two pounds. On today's market, silver runs about $100 a pound. So a tooth was worth between $34 and $66 in today's currency.

In Old Testament times, justice was determined by judges, not by the person injured (see Deuteronomy 19:18). Jewish writings from around Christ's time also gave guidance for damages.

At a time when people had a right to justice under the Law, Jesus told the people, "Do not resist an evil person. If someone strikes you on the right cheek, turn to him the other also" (Matthew 5:39).

That raises the tough and dangerous question: Did Jesus literally mean we should "not resist an evil person"?

Many Christians think so. They have interpreted this as a call to pacifism. They won't protect themselves when physically attacked, nor will they fight for family or country.

Others ask questions like these: If that is what Jesus is teaching, why did God give us such a powerful survival instinct? Why did Jesus escape from the crowd that tried to throw Him over a cliff (see Luke 4:30)? Why did Paul appeal to his rights as a Roman citizen when he was unjustly imprisoned, and why did he appeal to those same rights to keep Roman soldiers from beating him (see Acts 25:10-11; 22:25)?

Perhaps Jesus had something else in mind.

Look closely at His words: "If someone strikes you on the right cheek." If you're right-handed, as 90 percent of us are,* how do you hit another person, who is facing you, on their right cheek? Simple. With the back of your right hand. A blow like that is not to inflict injury as much as insult, especially in Bible times.

Most adults are not violently attacked often, if ever. Yet,

most of us are insulted from time to time. When someone snaps at us, we want to snap back.

Jesus is telling us that in situations like this, He prefers we bite our tongue, not our critical neighbor.

Give Till It Doesn't Hurt
(Matthew 5:40-42)

There are times we need to exercise our rights. There are also times we should set aside those rights; when, in so doing, we can show God's love to people.

Jesus illustrated this by talking about clothing. He said if someone sues you to take your tunic, give the person your cloak also. A tunic was a long, loose-fitting undergarment. A cloak was a more expensive, warm, outer garment. The homeless used it as a blanket at night. Jewish law said no one had the right to take it from another permanently (see Exodus 22:26).

Jesus is not saying we should give our money and possessions to everyone who asks us for them. Nevertheless, Jesus is certainly saying we are to cultivate an attitude of generosity. We should detach ourselves from our possessions so when we give something away, we don't feel like we're losing a right arm.

In a way, we're to give until we're so used to it that giving doesn't hurt anymore. We're to show others the generosity God has shown us.

I wish I had reflected that generosity one rainy afternoon when I was working my way through college. An elderly man with a sack of bottles stopped by the gas station where I worked. The thin, bent-over gentleman, on his way to the store to redeem the bottles, was unprepared for the rain. We chatted as he waited in vain for the rain to stop. He struck me as a man who had worked hard during his life, a man trying to stretch his money during his retirement. I thought about loaning him my jacket and asking him to drop it off at the station on his way back. But I didn't. I watched him walk up the hill, getting wet as the rain continued.

Jesus also taught that Christian kindness includes more than being generous with our legal rights. He said we're to go the extra mile. Roman soldiers had the right to order citizens of conquered nations to carry supplies for up to a mile. One soldier exercised this right when he ordered Simon of Cyrene to carry Jesus' cross. This was humiliating to the Jews. It reminded them that the Promised Land was no longer theirs. And, worse, that their fate was in the hands of a pagan nation rather than God.

There is practical wisdom in the advice of Jesus. It becomes clearer as we compare it with the teaching of Epictetus (ep-ik-TEET-us), a first-century Roman philosopher. "If there is a requisition [same Greek word Jesus used] and a soldier seizes your donkey, don't resist or grumble; for then you will get a beating and still lose your donkey."

Jesus, however, was teaching more than self-preservation. He taught the disarmament of hostility. Nothing disarms like a smile backed up by generosity. We can give others a glimpse of God's love when we set aside our rights and do more than the minimum.

Love People You Don't Like
(Matthew 5:43-48)

I once worked for a Christian who was not easy to like. I watched him mistakenly and harshly accuse people. When he learned he was wrong, he never apologized.

I watched him bully secretaries. I listened to him brag that he didn't care what members in an upcoming committee meeting wanted, he was the chairman. I saw him set aside both God's law and civil law by forcing people into early retirement.

There is no reason on earth to love a man like this. Yet, heaven commands it.

Perhaps it helps us if we remember that the man is still

just a Christian under construction. Maybe the man had a harsh life and was only beginning to trust others. Whatever the case, Jesus calls us to love him.

Are we to love him with the kind of emotionally-laden love we have for our family or close friends? Jesus didn't use the Greek word for that kind of love. He used *agapē*. It means unconquerable goodwill. No matter what the person does to us or to people we care about, we genuinely want God's best for him or her.

This kind of love doesn't spring from something as un-controllable as emotion; it comes out of a God-empowered decision we make. We *decide* to wish for the person's best. And we follow up this decision by praying for that to happen. I've found it's hard to hate someone I pray for.

Conclusion

Put all this together, and we begin to get an idea what Jesus was talking about when He said, "Be perfect" (5:48). Jesus didn't mean we are to be free of mistakes in our words and actions. Our Lord used this phrase to sum up what He had just finished saying.

The message: God doesn't retaliate when we hurt Him. God is generous toward us. And God loves us even when we're unlovable. So we become perfect, in the sense Jesus in-tended, the moment we decide to devote ourselves whole-heartedly to imitating God. Of course, this is only possible through the in-filling, cleansing power of the Holy Spirit.

This pays eternal dividends. Yet, for those of us who don't like waiting, it can pay off in the here and now. A Christian I know learned this.

Skip said his family was losing sleep because of a next-door neighbor's black Labrador. Black Jack was put outside every evening. He apparently didn't like it because he barked all hours of the night. Skip called the neighbor and talked politely about the problem. The dog still barked. Skip called the neighbor and talked not-so-politely about the problem.

The dog still barked. Skip and other neighbors filed a legal complaint. The dog still barked.

Summer mercifully ended, and Black Jack stayed indoors. When spring arrived, Skip's wife took over a plate of brownies. The dog has been quiet since.

Notes:

*Though only about 10 percent of the world population is left-handed, the percentage is even lower in Eastern cultures, where left-handedness is looked on as evil. *Encyclopedia of Neuroscience,* vol. 2 (Boston: Birkhauser, 1987), 480.

Word to Remember: *But I tell you: Love your enemies and pray for those who persecute you* (Matthew 5:44).

Coming up . . . Holy living isn't something you can plot on a chart or grade with A's, B's, and C's. It would be hard for us to measure how effective we are in helping others, controlling our destructive criticism, or loving our enemies. However, one area is easier to evaluate—our mastery over temptation.

All of us know when we are tempted; we see the bait dangling there in front of us. We know if we are attracted to the bait. And we know whether or not we bit. The bad news about temptation is there are a lot of lines in the water. Everywhere we turn, we find lures. The good news is no one forces the bait down our throats. We always have the freedom to say no to what is harmful for us and yes to what is good for us and the Kingdom.

1 Corinthians 10:1-14

14 ¹For I do not want you to be ignorant of the fact, brothers, that our forefathers were all under the cloud and that they all passed through the sea. ²They were all baptized into Moses in the cloud and in the sea. ³They all ate the same spiritual food ⁴and drank the same spiritual drink; for they drank from the spiritual rock that accompanied them, and that rock was Christ. ⁵Nevertheless, God was not pleased with most of them; their bodies were scattered over the desert.

⁶Now these things occurred as examples to keep us from setting our hearts on evil things as they did. ⁷Do not be idolaters, as some of them were; as it is written: "The people sat down to eat and drink and got up to indulge in pagan revelry." ⁸We should not commit sexual immorality, as some of them did—and in one day twenty-three thousand of them died. ⁹We should not test the Lord, as some of them did—and were killed by snakes. ¹⁰And do not grumble, as some of them did—and were killed by the destroying angel.

¹¹These things happened to them as examples and were written down as warnings for us, on whom the fulfillment of the ages has come. ¹²So, if you think you are standing firm, be careful that you don't fall! ¹³No temptation has seized you except what is common to man. And God is faithful; he will not let you be tempted beyond what you can bear. But when you are tempted, he will also provide a way out so that you can stand up under it.

¹⁴Therefore, my dear friends, flee from idolatry.

11

Warning: Temptation Ahead

HOW MUCH DO we learn from history?
Consider these answers from history students, collected by their teachers:

- Moses went up on Mount Cyanide to get the Ten Commandments. He died before he ever reached Canada.
- Adam and Eve were created from an apple tree. One of their children, Cain, asked, "Am I my brother's son?"
- Homer was not written by Homer, but by another man of that name.
- Socrates died from an overdose of wedlock.
- Magna Carta provided that no man should be hanged twice for the same offense.
- Martin Luther was nailed to the church door at Wittenberg for selling papal indulgences. He died a horrible death, being excommunicated by a bull.*

How much do we learn from history? Apparently, not enough.

So what's new? Paul discovered this in first-century Corinth. Some of the Christians there thought they could do as they pleased since they were baptized and had taken communion. Because they figured their membership in God's kingdom couldn't be canceled, they thought it wouldn't do any harm to enjoy the good food and bawdy fun at banquets held in honor of heathen gods.

They came to the wrong conclusion, as we will see.

Adjust Your Rearview Mirror
(1 Corinthians 10:1-5)

Paul went to work on an iceberg of a problem. Floating above water was the tiny tip: the problem of Christians eating meat offered to idols. These believers thought that since they had observed the rituals of baptism and the Lord's Supper, they could safely enjoy party-time banquets featuring meat sacrificed to idols.

Lurking under the surface floated the remaining 85 percent of the iceberg: the problem of spiritual over-confidence. Let's give the Corinthians the benefit of the doubt. Let's assume they weren't practicing an early version of the belief that once we belong to God, He won't disown us no matter what we do. If they didn't believe this, they at least felt they could handle the temptations at the feasts. After all, they were special people. Baptism symbolized their cleansing from their old life, and they had been resurrected to new life, as shown by the emblems of Christ's body and blood.

Paul took the Corinthians back to the Exodus to remind them that even God's elite can fall. God's chosen people were, in a sense, baptized. They passed through the Red Sea and left their old lives of slavery behind them. And they, too, were raised and nourished into new life through heaven-sent provisions. They ate manna, which Paul compared to Christ's body. And they drank water that miraculously sprang from a rock, which Paul compared to Christ's blood.

Wherever the Hebrews went, God and His provision went. The manna and water followed them, as evidence God himself led them. Jews and godly Gentiles in Paul's day knew well a Jewish legend about the water-yielding rock. Tradition said that after the water sprang out of the rock, the rock followed the Hebrews to provide them with water. Paul didn't endorse this legend, but he used the readers' awareness of it to symbolize that God was with the chosen people as surely as He was with the Corinthians.

So the Corinthians were a bit like the chosen people. Now comes the clincher: The chosen people died in the desert. Every person over 20 years of age from that temptation-tripped generation died, except Joshua and Caleb (see Numbers 14:29-30).

Paul's message was clear: Adjust your rearview mirror. Take a good look at what has happened to others in the past. Learn from their mistakes.

Count the Bodies Along the Road
(1 Corinthians 10:6-10)

If a Roman had walked up to a Corinthian Christian and said, "Come with me and worship Jupiter," the Corinthian would likely have said something comparable to a phrase popular a few years ago, "No way, José." Yet, temptation usually isn't that obvious. Temptation says, "Let's go for a walk" without telling you you're headed toward the heathen temples on Mount Olympus. Still, Paul knew where the Corinthian Christians were headed.

As far as the apostle was concerned, there was nothing wrong with simply eating meat that had been offered to idols. Pagan priests sold most of the sacrificed meat to local butchers, who sold it at the market. You couldn't always tell the idol-meat from the other meat. Merchants didn't label it, "20 Percent Off—Sacrificed Meat" or "Premium Kosher." Paul's advice: buy the meat and don't ask questions. However, eating this meat at feasts that honored false gods was another matter (see 1 Corinthians 10:25-30).

Serious pagan worshipers believed the god they were honoring with the banquet was a real, though invisible, guest at the party. In addition, they believed the god entered the meat of the sacrificed animal, then entered the person who ate the meat. Paul didn't believe spirits of any kind could enter and possess Christians in this way. Yet, he certainly believed that being around others who did believe it could undermine the faith of some Christians—especially the spiritually immature and the over-confident.

These banquets featured another kind of temptation that wasn't so subtle. The festivities could degenerate into drunken orgies, featuring erotic dancers and cult prostitutes, designed to excite the gods sexually. It's unlikely the gods were excited, but those at the banquet sure were. Corinth, with many pagan temples in Paul's day, had a reputation for such practices.

It was a similar idol-worshiping orgy that the wandering Hebrews had with the Moabites. Apparently, about 23,000 Israelites sinned. Their punishment, death.

Paul also cited other times the Hebrews fell victim to temptation. During their wanderings, they pushed God too far by whining about not having enough food and water. In spite of the miracles He performed for them, they burst into complaint about what He wasn't doing instead of praise for what He had done and would do. You can read about it in Numbers 21:4-9. Many complainers died at the bite of poisonous snakes.

We're not sure what grumblers Paul referred to in verse 10. It might be the folks in Numbers 11:1-3. Yet, Paul's point is clear. One example of temptation is the temptation to complain about God. It is more than just saying something pessimistic like, "You know bad things are going to happen; they always do." Rather it goes on to revile the faithfulness of God. That sort of focusing on the negative, at the exclusion of the positive, is sin.

Temptation is out there, waiting to ambush us. It wears many disguises. And it's deadly.

Count Your Blessings You're Not One of Them
(1 Corinthians 10:11-12)

This tragic history is recorded not to show the world how weak the Hebrews were, but how powerful temptation is.

Nothing can immunize human beings from temptation. Not rebirth. Not entire sanctification. In fact, spiritual growth seems to attract temptation in the same way moths

are drawn to light. And I don't know of anything more invit-
ing to temptation than spiritual cockiness. That's the disease
the Corinthians suffered.

Their spiritual self-confidence must have been a bit like
the military self-confidence of the people in New Tyre. They
heard Alexander the Great was coming, so they abandoned
their city of old Tyre, moved to a nearby island half a mile into the Mediterranean, and built thick walls around their new
town. When Alexander arrived and ordered them to surren-
der, they laughed. However, Alexander laughed last. He tore
down the remains of old Tyre and used it to build a causeway
to the island. He destroyed the new city and its people.

One way or another, temptation will reach us. Of
course, that doesn't mean we have to go looking for it, as the
Corinthians did.

When we face temptation and are able to resist it, we
should count our blessings. Many before us have not resisted.

Follow the Map and Drive On
(I Corinthians 10:13-14)

The bad news is that no matter where we go or what we
do, we will eventually find ourselves nose-to-nose with
temptation.

The good news is that God gives us directions for steer-
ing clear of many temptations. He gives us specific instructions in His Word for dealing with the ones we inevitably
face, and He promises to make a way of escape for us.

The image Paul creates is that of a person trapped in the
mountains and surrounded by a war party. For the trapped
person, God provides a mountain pass.

Given the intensity of temptations I've faced, I picture
something more miraculous. I picture myself trapped in a
box canyon. Behind me, and from the other side of the
canyon, God is chiseling an escape route through solid rock.
And the moment I turn around to Him, light breaks through
the wall and I'm saved.

Perhaps you would prefer to think of a cavalry showing up at just the right moment to scatter your enemies. That's a good image, because as sure as the cavalry arrives in a nick of time in old westerns, God is always there when we need Him.

Paul's point: No temptation is irresistible.

In every temptation, when we turn to God, we find victory.

I read about a primitive tribe in New Zealand that encouraged its warriors to eat the first enemy they killed. They believed that in doing this, warriors gained strength from the defeated foe.

Though we don't believe the tribal superstition, it illustrates what happens when we defeat temptation. We grow stronger and more capable of overcoming temptation in the future. We are never capable enough to overcome them on our own, but God doesn't ask that.

Notes:

*Richard Lederer, *Anguished English* (Charleston, S.C.: Wyrick and Co., 1987), 10.

Word to Remember: *No temptation has seized you except what is common to man. And God is faithful; he will not let you be tempted beyond what you can bear. But when you are tempted, he will also provide a way out so that you can stand up under it* (1 Corinthians 10:13).

Coming up . . . It's not always easy to live on earth by heaven's rules. Sin runs wild on this planet. So while we have God's Spirit within us nudging us heavenward, we have sinners around us urging us to follow them every direction but up. These people live by the "me first" motto. They rarely sacrifice their time or money for others. They have mastered the tongue as a butcher's tool. They don't get mad; they get even. They don't bother resisting many temptations because the pleasure seems to outweigh the price. In spite of all these negative models, God calls us to follow His model. And because we're only human and can't consistently obey Him in our own strength, He helps us in our weakness.

2 Corinthians 4:7-15

4 ⁷But we have this treasure in jars of clay to show that this all-surpassing power is from God and not from us. ⁸We are hard pressed on every side, but not crushed; perplexed, but not in despair; ⁹persecuted, but not abandoned; struck down, but not destroyed. ¹⁰We always carry around in our body the death of Jesus, so that the life of Jesus may also be revealed in our body. ¹¹For we who are alive are always being given over to death for Jesus' sake, so that his life may be revealed in our mortal body. ¹²So then, death is at work in us, but life is at work in you.

¹³It is written: "I believed; therefore I have spoken." With that same spirit of faith we also believe and therefore speak, ¹⁴because we know that the one who raised the Lord Jesus from the dead will also raise us with Jesus and present us with you in his presence. ¹⁵All this is for your benefit, so that the grace that is reaching more and more people may cause thanksgiving to overflow to the glory of God.

Galatians 2:11-14, 20

2 ¹¹When Peter came to Antioch, I opposed him to his face, because he was clearly in the wrong. ¹²Before certain men came from James, he used to eat with the Gentiles. But when they arrived, he began to draw back and separate himself from the Gentiles because he was afraid of those who belonged to the circumcision group. ¹³The other Jews joined him in his hypocrisy, so that by their hypocrisy even Barnabas was led astray.

¹⁴When I saw that they were not acting in line with the truth of the gospel, I said to Peter in front of them all, "You are a Jew, yet you live like a Gentile and not like a Jew. How is it, then, that you force Gentiles to follow Jewish customs? . . . ²⁰I have been crucified with Christ and I no longer live, but Christ lives in me. The life I live in the body, I live by faith in the Son of God, who loved me and gave himself for me.

12

We're Only Human

AS EARLY AS the time of Noah, the Lord began to restrict the diet of His covenant people. A distinction was made between clean and unclean animals to be taken into the ark. After the Flood, the Lord instructed His people not to drink blood because it represented life (Genesis 9:4).

The primary revelation from God to His people concerning food is found in Leviticus 11. Five categories of living things were regulated: an animal, to be acceptable, had to have completely divided split hooves and chew its cud. Sea life had to have fins and scales. Birds could not be predators nor scavengers. Winged insects were forbidden, except for locusts and grasshoppers. Animals that "move on the ground" like reptiles and rodents were prohibited.

The dietary laws were part of broader regulations on how to live the holy life. There are some hygienic reasons for restricting some food. Pagan practice, such as boiling a young goat in its mother's milk, ruled out others. However, the primary reason for the dietary rules was to set Israel off from the rest of humankind and establish it as a holy nation. These rules, as the study of this chapter reveals, became a point of tension in the early New Testament church.

I'm Only Human

We do stupid things—on occasion. When our conscience, or worse, a witness, chides us, we sometimes reply, "I'm only human."

My son was two months old when I did a human, stupid thing. It was 3:30 in the morning. My wife was working the night shift as a hospital nurse. Bradley woke up crying. I calmed him down, but he refused to go back to bed. Each time I laid him down, either in his bed or beside me, he began crying again. I changed him, fed him, burped him, gave him medicine. He still cried.

Finally, in utter frustration, helplessness, and bleary-eyed anger, I swatted him twice on his padded behind. Not hard enough to hurt his bottom, double dipped in diapers. But the thunderclaps scared him to newer and higher pitches.

It does absolutely no good to swat a two-month-old. It only hurt him and me.

We're all human, every one of us, but that doesn't mean we are necessarily hopeless—not if Christ lives in us. If we let Him, He can take our flaws and change them one by one.

It's true. We're human. Yet, as we will see in this chapter, God lives in us, uses us, and refines us.

God Lives in Us
(2 Corinthians 4:7-15)

We usually put treasures in appropriate containers. Stocks and bonds in safety deposit boxes. Fresh-brewed gourmet coffee in china cups. Jewelry in hand-carved mahogany boxes.

Yet, look where God put His treasure on this earth—in people like Paul and you and me. The apostle wrote to the struggling Corinthian church, "We have this treasure in jars of clay" (4:7). Perhaps Paul was making a comparison to clay pots that people in his day hid money in and buried near their houses. Or, given what Paul said in verse 6 about letting light shine in darkness, perhaps he was contrasting Christians to the plain-looking clay lamps that lit houses and synagogues.

In either case, Paul's point is that God has entrusted the Good News to flawed messengers.

Take Paul, for example. His critics said, "His letters are weighty and forceful, but in person he is unimpressive and his speaking amounts to nothing" (2 Corinthians 10:10). A letter from the second century describes Paul as a bald-headed, bowlegged, short man, with a big nose and one long eyebrow that lay across his forehead like a dead caterpillar.

In spite of his weaknesses, the power of God lived in him. He illustrated this by citing evidence from his life. Paul was:

"hard pressed . . . , but not crushed;

perplexed, but not in despair;

persecuted, but not abandoned;

struck down, but not destroyed" (4:8).

Paul had been publicly beaten at least eight times. Five of those times the Jews gave him 39 lashes from a whip, for a total of 195. The Romans also beat him three times with a rod. He was stoned in one city and left for dead. He was shipwrecked three times. And he was imprisoned no less than five times—probably more.

The apostle faced death regularly. Eventually, it would snare his body. Still, the suffering and death Paul endured brought hope and eternal life to the Corinthians and all who heard and responded to the message Paul shared.

With Christ in us we, too, can overcome our humanity. Shipwrecked, we become Paul, looking for the next boat out. Put us in a concentration camp, we become Corrie ten Boom. With one of our arms crippled, we become David Livingstone. With a broken neck, we become Joni Eareckson Tada. Surrounded by poverty, we become Mother Teresa.

Even throw a crying baby in our laps, and we learn to sleep in rocking chairs.

God Uses Us
(Galatians 2:11-14)

Even the first Christians were all-too-human. The Bible doesn't gloss over the mistakes they made. When we look at Peter, we know we're not looking at Super Christian. We're looking at a man who was probably reminded every morning when the roosters crowed that he had denied Jesus. Yet, God still used him.

In this passage, we see how God used Paul to adjust Peter's actions. We also see a confused, perhaps even hypocritical man, whom God continued to use in spite of his repeated inconsistency.

Paul and Barnabas had planted the world's first Gentile church in Antioch. Peter apparently came for an extended visit. While there, he ate with and enjoyed the company of non-Jewish Christians.

Then some other visitors arrived—ultraconservative Jewish Christians from Jerusalem. They believed Jesus was the Messiah, all right. However, they also followed Jewish laws, which God had given through Moses to keep His chosen people from being absorbed into the pagan religions surrounding them.

Circumcision, cleansing rituals, and laws about what they could eat separated Jews from others. Strict Jews would not even do business with Gentiles, let alone eat with them. Peter, Paul, and Barnabas believed the coming of Jesus fulfilled God's covenant with Israel and replaced the Jewish laws with a new covenant. The new covenant called people beyond rules and toward principles. Principles like loving God with all your heart and others as yourself.

Peter was the first person God called to preach to the "unclean" Gentiles, whom God said were no longer unclean (see Acts 10).

Somehow, the visiting Jews convinced Peter and Barnabas to stop eating the churchwide meal with Gentile Christians. Perhaps the two leaders were simply trying to keep the peace by skipping the shared meals while the Jews were in town. "Peace at any price," we might call it. Paul wasn't willing to pay that price.

The price tag required Christians to stop eating together and enjoying fellowship. It set up a caste system with two levels: "common" Christians (Gentile believers who didn't observe Jewish customs), and "super" Christians (Jewish believers).

We don't know if this clash took place before or after

the Jerusalem Council, recorded in Acts 15. In either case, it makes us wonder how solid was this Peter, whose name means "rock." At the Council, as well as after the Acts 10 vision that led Peter to baptize a Gentile centurion, the apostle stood firm in his support of Gentile Christians. Yet here in Antioch, he faltered and fled. And he took pastor Barnabas with him.

We can only imagine how hurt the Gentile Christians must have been when they saw one of their pastors and one of Jesus' apostles turn their backs on them.

Still, God, at work in Paul, resolved the issue with a difficult face-to-face meeting between the ministers. And God, at work in Peter and Barnabas, helped them respond by admitting their mistake. We know this because both continued ministering to Gentiles and teaching salvation through faith, not through following Jewish customs.

God Refines Us
(Galatians 2:20)

Paul knew what it was like to live by the Jewish law. He had been a Pharisee, a branch of Judaism that prided itself in following the Law. It was false pride.

God gave the Law to help identify the Jewish people as His chosen instrument for bringing salvation to the world. The Law was not a merit program, through which people could earn badges so they could deserve to stand before God. Even if it were, no one could complete the program, for no human could faithfully obey all of the laws all of the time.

The Law left Paul feeling like a failure. He told the Romans, "I have the desire to do what is good, but I cannot carry it out. For what I do is not the good I want to do" (Romans 7:18-19).

Nevertheless, Paul said he was no longer a slave to the Law or sin. He had been freed through his crucifixion with Christ. The old Paul was dead. A new Paul was alive as surely as the resurrected Christ lived.

Paul was saying that when he accepted Jesus into his life as Messiah, his outlook and goals began to change. It transformed his question from "What should *I* do?" to "What would *Christ* want me to do?"

The apostle didn't lose his individuality. He still had the freedom to make decisions—and mistakes—like his friend Peter. However, his love of Jesus left him wanting to please Jesus.

Conclusion

I remember reading about Tygranes (TY-gran-ees), a prince in Armenia when Cyrus of Persia conquered the land. The prince and his wife stood before Cyrus as the king sentenced the couple to death. The prince pleaded to receive double torture so his wife could be freed. Cyrus was so moved that he freed them both.

Later, the prince asked his wife what she thought of the mighty conqueror. "I gave no thought to him at all," she said. "I thought only of the man who was willing to bear the torture and the agony of death for me."

That kind of love changes people.

Word to Remember: *But we have this treasure in jars of clay to show that this all-surpassing power is from God and not from us* (2 Corinthians 4:7).

Coming up ... Other people can influence the way we think and behave. It's the "garbage in, garbage out" theory. Yet, as convincing as sinful people can be, we have to live among them. In fact, as Christians we are to take the message of salvation to them.

How do we counterbalance the negative influence they can have on us—the temptation to convert to their lifestyle instead of converting them to a godly lifestyle?

The answer is in this chapter: We spend time with heaven's kin. You might call it the "treasure in, treasure out" theory. We draw strength from the times of deep sharing we spend with God and His people. In those moments of intimate fellowship, we can find power for holy living.

1 John 1:1—2:6, 9-10

1 [1]That which was from the beginning, which we have heard, which we have seen with our eyes, which we have looked at and our hands have touched—this we proclaim concerning the Word of life. [2]The life appeared; we have seen it and testify to it, and we proclaim to you the eternal life, which was with the Father and has appeared to us. [3]We proclaim to you what we have seen and heard, so that you also may have fellowship with us. And our fellowship is with the Father and with his Son, Jesus Christ. [4]We write this to make our joy complete.

[5]This is the message we have heard from him and declare to you: God is light; in him there is no darkness at all. [6]If we claim to have fellowship with him yet walk in the darkness, we lie and do not live by the truth. [7]But if we walk in the light, as he is in the light, we have fellowship with one another, and the blood of Jesus, his Son, purifies us from all sin.

[8]If we claim to be without sin, we deceive ourselves and the truth is not in us. [9]If we confess our sins, he is faithful and just and will forgive us our sins and purify us from all unrighteousness. [10]If we claim we have not sinned, we make him out to be a liar and his word has no place in our lives.

2 [1]My dear children, I write this to you so that you will not sin. But if anybody does sin, we have one who speaks to the Father in our defense—Jesus Christ, the Righteous One. [2]He is the atoning sacrifice for our sins, and not only for ours but also for the sins of the whole world.

[3]We know that we have come to know him if we obey his commands. [4]The man who says, "I know him," but does not do what he commands is a liar, and the truth is not in him. [5]But if anyone obeys his word, God's love is truly made complete in him. This is how we know we are in him: [6]Whoever claims to live in him must walk as Jesus did.

. . . [9]Anyone who claims to be in the light but hates his brother is still in the darkness. [10]Whoever loves his brother lives in the light, and there is nothing in him to make him stumble.

13

Fellowship Beyond Friendship

THE SINGLE, MOST important reason adults come to Sunday School is to study the Bible. So concludes a recent study of North American Sunday Schools by the Christian Education department of a Christian college.

Nevertheless, fellowship placed a close second.

"Fellowship for the early Christians was more than our chitchat around Cokes and chips, or coffee and doughnuts. Fellowship in the Early Church meant sharing at an intimate level in the joys and pains of another."*

First John grapples with the issue of Christian fellowship. The letter was written to the remnant of a group of Christians that had split apart. Both the group that left and those that remained needed a refresher course on fellowship with God and with other believers.

John, son of Zebedee and brother of James, was one of the closest apostles to Jesus. He was among the first to be called to follow the Master, and was invited to witness special events, such as the Transfiguration.

Very early traditions say that John ministered in the Roman province of Asia and its leading city of Ephesus. His move there may have come as a result of the outbreak of the Jewish War in A.D. 66. Sometime during the reign of the Roman Emperor Domitian (dah-MISH-an, A.D. 81-96), he was exiled on the island of Patmos, where he wrote the revelation he received from the Lord.

The Gospel of John was likely written about A.D. 85, the letters shortly thereafter. If John was about 25 years of age when Jesus died, he would have been nearly 60 when he arrived in Ephesus. If he returned to Ephesus after exile on Patmos, as tradition suggests, he would have been at least 90 when he died. Thus, he was the last of the original Twelve to die, and perhaps the only one who was not martyred. Except, of course, for Judas Iscariot, who committed suicide.

So John, who lived a long life as a Christian, was most qualified to discuss all the aspects of Christian fellowship.

Where It Starts

(1 John 1:1-5)

Christian fellowship begins with a holy God who reached out to disobedient humans. He made the first move. He built the bridge to us.

In doing this, He opened the way for communication between himself and us. Thus, He gave us a model to follow in our fellowship with others.

The Christians who seceded from the church faced more than the loss of fellowship with the believers they left behind. Because our relationship with Jesus is so closely related to how well we get along with other Christians, they were in danger of sinning.

The problem revolved around a couple of heresies they were touting. *First, they taught that Jesus didn't really come in the flesh.* God, they said, would not soil His holiness by taking on our humanity. For them, Jesus was a kind of ghostly image that only appeared human. A later generation of the Church called this unorthodox teaching Docetism (DOE-sa-tiz-um), from a Greek word that means "to seem" or "to appear."

John replies to this heresy by saying he heard, looked at, and touched Jesus. The disciple's words echo those of the resurrected Christ to the Eleven. "Touch me and see; a ghost does not have flesh and bones, as you see I have" (Luke 24:39).

The second heresy of the splinter group was that they thought their faith in God made them eternally safe. Sin could not fracture their relationship with Him. The body, they taught, was like a tent that covered the spirit. Since they argued that the body could not contaminate the spirit, it didn't matter what sins the body committed. As long as believers held on to their faith, their salvation was secure.

We see this same heresy today in people who claim to know God, yet who see no need for the Cross, for forgiveness, or for holy living. With words, they say they know God. With actions, they prove they don't. They speak of living with enlightenment, yet walk in darkness.

God's redemptive work, His reaching out to people who were stumbling around in darkness, creates more than a fellowship between himself and the people who accept Him and follow His leading. It establishes a community of fellow travelers in the light. We share the same Lord, the same deliverance from darkness, and the same journey toward eternity.

"Fellowship" is from a Greek word that means far more than enjoying the company of one another, certainly more than savoring hot coffee and donuts together, though social times are important. The Greek word is *koinonia* (koy-no-NEE-ah). Words like these have been used to translate it: generosity, participation, sharing, and partnership. It means belonging to one another, depending on each other. It expresses the most intimate kinds of relationships, such as marriage.

Genuine fellowship with God is not limited to quick prayers over fast food, or three-minute devotions on the pillow as we slip into slumber. Genuine fellowship with believers means taking the time to learn where people hurt and what they need, then doing something about it. In the Early Church, believers went so far as to sell some of their goods to help their needy brothers and sisters (Acts 2:44-45).

A young couple I know paid a semester's tuition for a ministerial student in seminary. The couple decided to help when they heard the student and his family had suffered some financial setbacks. They were planning to drop out of school and look for a church to pastor. The gift encouraged the student to finish his last year of school.

That's fellowship. It started with God's outstretched hand. Then it expressed itself with a human's outstretched hand.

Where It Stops
(1 John 1:6—2:2)

Christian fellowship ends where disobedience to God begins.

The splinter group was wrong. Sin does make a difference in a person's relationship with God as well as with others. Sin blows apart the bridge God built to us. It rips holes in the Christlike bridges we have built to other believers.

John says it well. God, our Source of fellowship, is light. "If we claim to have fellowship with him yet walk in the darkness, we lie" (1:6).

Our words need to match our actions.

"Walk in the light, as he is in the light" (1:7) means we should follow the guidance of the Lord. "Walk" is in the present tense. It identifies a continuing way of life.

This doesn't mean Christians have lost the ability to sin. God does not take away our ability to sin; He gives us the power not to sin.

If we sin, we are not to do as the splinter group in John's day did. We are not to deny it. We are to confess it, find forgiveness, and receive power to resist temptation in the future. John himself said, "My dear children, I write this to you so that you will not sin" (2:1).

The tone and selection of these words paint the picture of a saintly church father speaking to young believers. By the time John wrote this letter, he was an old man—perhaps the last of the Twelve who had walked with Jesus.

The point is clear. Sin is not an inevitable part of the Christian walk. We don't have to spend our lives exploding holes in bridges of fellowship, then patching up the holes. Christ's sacrifice not only provides forgiveness for past sins but also it gives us the strength to live holy lives day by day.

Disobedience undermines our fellowship with God. When we lose touch with Him, when we start to drift out into the shadows, we lose touch with the community of light.

How to Spell It
(I John 2:3-6, 9-10)

It takes only four letters to spell Christian fellowship: l-o-v-e.

Love God, and show it by obeying Him.

Love others, and show it by helping them.

"The man who says, 'I know him,' but does not do what he commands is a liar" (2:4). If we know God, we will try to live as obediently toward Him as Jesus did when He walked the earth.

"Anyone who claims to be in the light but hates his brother is still in the darkness" (2:9). Since John is addressing the remnant of a Christian community that split in half, "brother" probably refers to other professing Christians. Still, that doesn't mean we should show any less love to our non-Christian neighbors. It was Jesus who said we should love our neighbors as ourselves.

I enjoy chitchat with Christian friends. Cup in hand, I talk about football, ice storms, or politics. For me, that is fellowship in first gear.

I also need fellowship in overdrive.

I can't remember what I chatted about during the coffee and doughnut time in Sunday School last week. Yet, I remember what happened in mid-January of 1988, when the flu came to visit at our home.

My wife got so sick the doctor admitted her to the hospital on Sunday afternoon.

The next morning the rest of us woke up sick—my five-month-old son, my two-year-old daughter, and me. Fever and exhaustion ruled the house. I was so weary I was barely able to change my boy's diapers. Each time I hit the living room couch, I dematerialized. Fortunately for me, the kids were just as weary.

My wife called the church office to ask for prayer, but we got much more than that. She got visits in the hospital. And I got food-laden, help-offering visits at home.

A woman who worked with my wife in the church nursery brought over chicken-noodle soup, gelatin, and lemon-lime soda. Two ladies from our Sunday School class brought over a big meal of noodles, homemade potpie, and gourmet ice cream. In addition, a nurse in our class offered to come over and take care of the kids while I slept. I turned her down because I didn't want to contaminate her family; she had a little boy my daughter's age.

This is Christian fellowship at its best. It started with God reaching out to people. It journeys toward completion as we reach out to others, and as we allow others to reach out to us.

Notes:

*Jerry McCant, "How God Grew a Church," *Illustrated Bible Life,* (September, October, November, 1990): 44.

Word to Remember: *But if anyone obeys his word, God's love is truly made complete in him. This is how we know we are in him: Whoever claims to live in him must walk as Jesus did* (1 John 2:5-6).

Appendix

The following doctrinal statements about entire sanctification are presented for those who wish to explore this biblical theme further. A listing of scripture passages relating to the topic follows the statements. The listing is not meant to be exhaustive, but merely representative of the Bible's teaching about holiness.

Church of the Nazarene
X. Entire Sanctification

13. We believe that entire sanctification is that act of God, subsequent to regeneration, by which believers are made free from original sin, or depravity, and brought into a state of entire devotement to God, and the holy obedience of love made perfect.

It is wrought by the baptism with the Holy Spirit, and comprehends in one experience the cleansing of the heart from sin and the abiding, indwelling presence of the Holy Spirit, empowering the believer for life and service.

Entire sanctification is provided by the blood of Jesus, is wrought instantaneously by faith, preceded by entire consecration; and to this work and state of grace the Holy Spirit bears witness.

This experience is also known by various terms representing its different phases, such as "Christian perfection," "perfect love," "heart purity," "the baptism with the Holy Spirit," "the fullness of the blessing," and "Christian holiness."

14. We believe that there is a marked difference between a pure heart and a mature character. The former is obtained in an instant, the result of entire sanctification; the latter is the result of growth in grace.

We believe that the grace of entire sanctification includes the impulse to grow in grace. However, this impulse must be consciously nurtured, and careful attention given to the requisites and processes of spiritual development and improvement in Christlikeness of character and personality. Without such purposeful endeavor one's witness may be impaired and the grace itself frustrated and ultimately lost.

—*Manual/2001-2005*

The Wesleyan Church

XIV. Sanctification: Initial, Progressive, Entire

236. We believe that sanctification is that work of the Holy Spirit by which the child of God is separated from sin unto God and is enabled to love God with all the heart and to walk in all His holy commandments blameless. Sanctification is initiated at the moment of justification and regeneration. From that moment there is a gradual or progressive sanctification as the believer walks with God and daily grows in grace and in a more perfect obedience to God. This prepares for the crisis of entire sanctification which is wrought instantaneously when believers present themselves as living sacrifices, holy and acceptable to God, through faith in Jesus Christ, being effected by the baptism with the Holy Spirit who cleanses the heart from all inbred sin. The crisis of entire sanctification perfects the believer in love and empowers that person for effective service. It is followed by lifelong growth in grace and the knowledge of our Lord and Savior Jesus Christ. The life of holiness continues through faith in the sanctifying blood of Christ and evidences itself by loving obedience to God's revealed will.

—*The Discipline, 1996*

The Free Methodist Church

XII. Entire Sanctification

A/119. Entire sanctification is that work of the Holy Spirit, subsequent to regeneration, by which the fully consecrated believers, upon exercise of faith in the atoning blood of Christ, are cleansed in that moment from all inward sin and empowered for service. The resulting relationship is attested by the witness of the Holy Spirit and is maintained by faith and obedience. Entire sanctification enables believers to love God with all their hearts, souls, strength, and minds, and their neighbor as themselves, and it prepares them for greater growth in grace.

—*1999 Book of Discipline*

Scriptures

General

Jeremiah 31:31-34
Ezekiel 36:25-27
Malachi 3:2-3
Matthew 3:11-12
Luke 3:16-17
John 7:37-39; 14:15-23; 17:6-20
Acts 1:5; 2:1-4; 15:8-9
Romans 6:11-13, 19; 8:1-4, 8-14; 12:1-2
2 Corinthians 6:14—7:1
Galatians 2:20; 5:16-25
Ephesians 3:14-21; 5:17-18, 25-27
Philippians 3:10-15
Colossians 3:1-17
1 Thessalonians 5:23-24
Hebrews 4:9-11; 10:10-17; 12:1-2; 13:12
1 John 1:7, 9

"Christian perfection" / "Perfect love"

Deuteronomy 30:6
Matthew 5:43-48; 22:37-40
Romans 12:9-21; 13:8-10
1 Corinthians 13
Philippians 3:10-15
Hebrews 6:1
1 John 4:17-18

"Heart purity"

Matthew 5:8
Acts 15:8-9
1 Peter 1:22
1 John 3:3

"Baptism with the Holy Spirit"

Jeremiah 31:31-34
Ezekiel 36:25-27
Malachi 3:2-3
Matthew 3:11-12

Luke 3:16-17
Acts 1:5; 2:1-4; 15:8-9

"Fullness of the blessing"

Romans 15:29

"Christian holiness"

Matthew 5:1—7:29
John 15:1-11
Romans 12:1—15:3
2 Corinthians 7:1
Ephesians 4:17—5:20
Philippians 1:9-11; 3:12-15
Colossians 2:20—3:17
1 Thessalonians 3:13; 4:7-8; 5:23
2 Timothy 2:19-22
Hebrews 10:19-25; 12:14; 13:20-21
1 Peter 1:15-16
2 Peter 1:1-11; 3:18
Jude 20-21

For Further Reading

The following bibliography is for those who wish to read further about the doctrine of holiness. This list represents only a fraction of the books that have been written on the subject. The books listed here can be purchased online at <www.nph.com> or by calling 1-800-877-0700.

Bassett, Paul. *Holiness Teaching: New Testament Times to Wesley.* Vol. 1 of *Great Holiness Classics.* Kansas City: Beacon Hill Press of Kansas City, 1997.

Dieter, Melvin E. *The 19th Century Holiness Movement.* Vol. 4 of *Great Holiness Classics.* Kansas City: Beacon Hill Press of Kansas City, 1998.

Dunning, H. Ray. *Grace, Faith and Holiness: A Wesleyan Systematic Theology.* Kansas City: Beacon Hill Press of Kansas City, 1988.

Greathouse, William M. *The Fullness of the Spirit.* Kansas City: Beacon Hill Press, 1958.

_____. *An Introduction to Wesleyan Theology (Revised).* Kansas City: Beacon Hill Press of Kansas City, 1989.

_____. *Love Made Perfect: Foundations for the Holy Life.* Kansas City: Beacon Hill Press of Kansas City, 1997.

_____. *Wholeness in Christ: Toward a Biblical Theology of Holiness.* Kansas City: Beacon Hill Press of Kansas City, 1998.

Harper, A. F. *Holiness Teaching Today.* Vol. 6 of *Great Holiness Classics.* Kansas City: Beacon Hill Press of Kansas City, 1987.

Knight, John A. *The Holiness Pilgrimage: Developing a Life-Style That Reflects Christ.* Kansas City: Beacon Hill Press of Kansas City, 1986.

_____. *All Loves Excelling: Proclaiming Our Wesleyan Message.* Kansas City: Beacon Hill Press of Kansas City, 1995.

Lyons, George. *Holiness in Everyday Life.* Kansas City: Beacon Hill Press of Kansas City, 1992.

_____. *More Holiness in Everyday Life.* Kansas City: Beacon Hill Press of Kansas City, 1997.

McCumber, W. E. *Holiness Preachers and Preaching.* Vol. 5 of *Great Holiness Classics.* Kansas City: Beacon Hill Press of Kansas City, 1989.

_____. *Love Conquers All: Essays on Holy Living.* Kansas City: Beacon Hill Press of Kansas City, 1992.

McKenna, David. *What a Time to Be Wesleyan: Proclaiming the Holiness Message with Passion and Purpose.* Kansas City: Beacon Hill Press of Kansas City, 1999.

Mitchell, T. Crichton. *The Wesley Century.* Vol. 2 of *Great Holiness Classics.* Kansas City: Beacon Hill Press of Kansas City, 1984.

Parrott, Leslie. *The Battle for Your Mind: Understanding the Sanctified Personality.* Kansas City: Beacon Hill Press of Kansas City, 1986.

_____. *What Is Sanctification? Understanding the Meaning of Entire Sanctification.* Kansas City: Beacon Hill Press, 1950.

Reed, Gerard. *C. S. Lewis and the Bright Shadow of Holiness.* Kansas City: Beacon Hill Press of Kansas City, 1999.

Rich, Marion K. *Song for All Seasons: Harmony in the Inner Life.* Kansas City: Beacon Hill Press of Kansas City, 1992.

Strait, C. Neil. *To Be Holy: Principles for Living the Spirit-Filled Life.* Kansas City: Beacon Hill Press of Kansas City, 1984.

Taylor, Richard S. *Leading Wesleyan Thinkers.* Vol. 3 of *Great Holiness Classics.* Kansas City: Beacon Hill Press of Kansas City, 1985.